yellowstone

Text by Erwin A. Bauer
Photographs by Erwin and Peggy Bauer

VOYAGEUR PRESS

Edited by Kathy Mallien
Cover designed by Leslie Dimond
Book designed by Helene Jones
Printed in Hong Kong
First hardcover edition 93 94 95 96 97 5 4 3 2 1
First softcover edition 94 95 96 97 98 5 4 3 2 1

Library of Congress Cataloging-in-Publication Data
Bauer, Erwin A.
    Yellowstone / text by Erwin A. Bauer ; photographs by Erwin and Peggy Bauer.
                    p.   cm.
    Includes bibliographical references.
    ISBN 0-89658-177-2
    ISBN 0-89658-248-5 (pbk.)
    1. Yellowstone National Park—Guidebooks. I. Bauer, Peggy.
    II. Title.
    F722.B39   1993
    917.87'520433—dc20   92-38044
                                        CIP

Published by
VOYAGEUR PRESS, INC.
P.O. Box 338, 123 North Second Street
Stillwater, MN 55082 U.S.A.
From Minnesota and Canada 612-430-2210
Toll-free 800-888-9653

Distributed in Canada by
RAINCOAST BOOKS
112 East 3rd Avenue
Vancouver, B.C. V5T 1C8

Voyageur Press books are also available at discounts for quantities for educational, fundraising, premium, or sales-promotion use. For details contact the marketing department. Please write or call for our free catalog of natural history publications.

CONTENTS

INTRODUCTION

My lifelong love affair with Yellowstone Park began when I was a very young man, in late springtime 1935, the morning after high school classes had adjourned. In the pre-dawn a young friend and I aimed a blue 1929 Dodge roadster westward from Cincinnati toward Wyoming. Our goal: Yellowstone National Park or bust. We had devoured all there was to read, over and over, about the park. But neither of us had ever been beyond Ohio's borders before.

We were poorly equipped and under-financed to travel anywhere, let alone across still-unpaved America. Nevertheless, during those Great Depression years, when gasoline cost twenty cents a gallon, we somehow made it to Yellowstone. And somehow, flat broke, I managed to land a job at the boat rental dock that existed near Fishing Bridge. I neglected to mention to my new employers that my sixteenth birthday was still two months away.

Until I married the person who shot many of the photographs in this book, I never spent a more glorious, more exciting, more revealing summer than that one. The work was menial; for about two dollars a ten-hour day I swabbed out dirty boats and dressed heavy strings of trout for visitors. Occasionally I rowed the rental boats for fishermen. Most nights I slept in a storage shed rolled up in ancient army blankets. Still, one golden day blended into another until suddenly it was September, and the park began to close down. It was also time to head homeward. Now, more than a half century later, I still remember what a bittersweet departure that was.

Other memories of that long-ago summer have never faded. I recall seeing a good many black bears, some of whom I met on the backcountry trails I hiked at every opportunity. There were grizzlies, too, and one day one of them swam across the Yellowstone River within sight of our boats. Another day while hiking the shore of Yellowstone Lake I came too abruptly upon a grizzly sow with twin cubs. The bruin woofed at me only once before all three ran away. I cannot recall a single incident between bears and people in the park, although they must have occurred.

I do not remember meeting many bison then; today they are the most easily seen of all wildlife in Yellowstone. The park then seemed to be swarming with travelers, but I realize there are twenty-five to thirty times as many on any July day now as in 1935. That summer also spoiled me. Never again—in Yellowstone or anywhere else—would I find fly fishing for trout to match what I found then in the Yellowstone River.

My career as a wildlife photographer also began that summer of '35 in Yellowstone. Far too much of my wages was spent on film for my Pilot, an early German reflex camera, even when I needed new hiking boots and a shirt. My main subjects were bears. I don't know what ever happened to those pictures—they weren't too bad, considering my equipment.

Eighteen years passed, and I fought in wars in Africa, Italy, and Korea. In 1953 I returned to Yellowstone and spent a month reexploring that magnificent real estate, hiking the trails I had tromped before as well as some new ones. Bears were as abundant as ever. In fact, it was difficult to drive far on park roads without meet-

Steep, turbulent Tower Creek races past hoodoos—strange, eroded rock formations—just above Tower Fall. A hiking trail leads from near here to the base of the falls.

The shrill bugling of a bull elk is clearly heard on a crisp September day, at the beginning of the elk's annual breeding season.

ing them, plenty of them, panhandling along the berms and causing "bear traffic jams."

Since 1953 I have visited Yellowstone at least once a year, most often in late summer and early autumn when the weather averages best, but in springtime and the dead of winter as well. During the 1960s Gene Wade, an outfitter from Cooke City, Montana, became a close friend and my Yellowstone backcountry mentor. On numerous pack trips on horseback we explored remote sections of the park difficult or impossible to reach in any other way. A typical expedition would take us completely across the Mirror Plateau or Specimen Ridge to see fossil forests of sycamore and oak, of walnut, magnolia, and dogwood trees buried millions of years ago and now exposed. We also broke camp and rode all morning through a snowstorm and white-out—on the Fourth of July.

Another summer we saddled up beside the southwest arm of Yellowstone Lake and then paralleled the Yellowstone River southward to the southeast corner of the park. There, some distance from the camp, standing waist-deep in Thorofare Creek with a trout on my line, I heard splashing behind me. Just a short cast away a grizzly stood erect, studying me. The next sound I heard was not the bear bounding away, but the pounding of my own heart.

Today Peggy and I live in Paradise Valley, the local and most descriptive name for the Yellowstone River valley, in south-central Montana. We are an easy hour's drive north of the park's north entrance. The Absaroka Range of the Rocky Mountains that looms high above (and east of) our home is the same mass of mountain wilderness that rises all along the eastern flank of the national park. So we spend a lot of time there—probably much more time than might seem necessary.

The truth is that Yellowstone Country has always been indelible in my psyche and always will be. In a lifetime devoted to vagabonding the earth's wild places, I have never found a place to exactly match this one, or a better place to return to.

GALLATIN NATIONAL FOREST

Gardiner

Cooke City

Silver Gate

Mammoth Hot Springs

Mount Everts

Yellowstone River

Gardner River

Tower-Roosevelt

TROUT LAKE

Indian Creek

Sheepeater Cliff

Tower Fall

Tower Falls

Pebble Creek

LAMAR VALLEY

Lamar River

Tower Creek

GRAND CANYON OF THE YELLOWSTONE RIVER

Mount Washburn

Virginia Cascades

MADISON VALLEY

Norris Geyser Basin

Canyon Village

MIRROR PLATEAU

Norris

Inspiration Point

West Yellowstone

Artist Point

Madison

Gibbon River

Lower Falls

Gibbon Falls

Upper Falls

Madison River

Nez Perce Creek

Alum Creek

Sulphur Caldron

LeHardy Rapids

SHOSHONE NATIONAL FOREST

Firebole River

CENTRAL

HAYDEN VALLEY

Fishing Bridge

Lake Village

Lower Geyser Basin

Fountain Paint Pot

PLATEAU

Midway Geyser Basin

Biscuit Basin

Upper Geyser Basin

ABSAROKA RANGE

Old Faithful

MADISON PLATEAU

SHOSHONE LAKE

YELLOWSTONE LAKE

LEWIS LAKE

HEART LAKE

Eagle Peak

Lewis River

Snake River

TARGHEE NATIONAL FOREST

Yellowstone River

BRIDGER-TETON NATIONAL FOREST

MONTANA

Yellowstone National Park

IDAHO

WYOMING

THE WORLD'S FIRST NATIONAL PARK

Soon after he was elected president, Ulysses S. Grant sent one of his young generals, Henry Washburn, to be surveyor-general of the distant Montana Territory. Not yet forty years old, Washburn was a lawyer, a former congressman from Indiana, and a restless soul. In Montana he met a kindred spirit, one Nathaniel P. Langford, a banker, former collector of internal revenue, and champion of the Northern Pacific Railway, which was busy bringing people and commerce into the territory. Both men were intrigued by the fantastic tales of Yellowstone Country and they decided to see it for themselves.

Thus, on August 22, 1870, Washburn and Langford set out on an expedition from Fort Ellis, near modern Bozeman, Montana. The trip would have much greater historical significance than either could possibly foresee. Accompanied by two merchants, a tax assessor, a judge, and a railroad official, along with a military escort commanded by Lieutenant Gustavus C. Doane, they marched southward until they reached what is now the northwestern corner of Wyoming.

Beyond that point the party entered a strange new world they simply could not believe. They scaled mountain peaks and descended into polychrome canyons. They climbed cliffs of "glass" (obsidian, really) and discovered boiling cauldrons around which the earth trembled, all the while watching for "unfriendly Indians." Trouble haunted them. Except for game trails the land was trackless, and there were bitter personal disputes. Men and horses were lost, and often the weather turned foul.

One party member, assessor Truman C. Everts, became separated from the group along the southern shore of Yellowstone Lake. His horse made off with his gun, blanket, matches, and other survival necessities, even his eyeglasses, still in the saddlebags. Everts was left with only the clothing on his back, a predicament that meant disaster in that time and place. Washburn, Langford, and Doane searched for Everts for a week before giving up and moving on.

Despite the numerous problems, the party also found and named some of the most spectacular geysers (Beehive, Castle, Grotto, Giant, and Giantess) and thermal basins on the face of the earth. The men stood in awe above and beneath thundering waterfalls. They cooked many of their meals without building a fire, using instead the heat of the thermal waters. In diaries several admitted that their minds were spinning from the extraordinary adventure. One traveler recalled his days as "deep spiritual experiences."

Returning homeward one still evening in late September, Washburn and his party sat around a campfire near present-day Madison Junction in what is now Yellowstone National Park. The hardships of the trek were behind them, and the men were feeling mellower and more relaxed than they had in many weeks. According to the notes of Judge Cornelius Hedges, the party discussed the future of the strange and starkly exquisite land they had just traversed. Most concurred, according to Hedges, that this remarkable region should never be

Castle Geyser erupts on a summer evening, not far from Old Faithful Geyser and the Old Faithful Inn.

privately owned or exploited, but instead should be held in trust by the American government for all its citizens. Hedges urged each of his fellow travelers to strive toward that end. He probably was the first person ever to use the phrase *national park*.

That startling concept, of land as a national treasure and as an all-American park, was extremely radical for its time. The prevailing philosophy then, even more so than now, was that God gave us all land on earth to be used. But in the eastern United States there were faint, post–Civil War stirrings of a conservation ethic. A few Americans were growing weary of familiar rural landscapes being consumed by polluting industry and development. Henry David Thoreau (author of *Walden*) and Ralph Waldo Emerson wrote about saving swamps and forests and birds, and early western artist George Catlin, then gaining celebrity, stated that land in the West should be left in its natural state for the Native Americans and wild creatures who lived there. A vague new idea was gradually taking shape.

After the 1870 Yellowstone Expedition, Hedges and Langford wrote newspaper and magazine articles that were widely circulated in the East. Two years later, in one of the most outstanding acts of his otherwise unpopular administration, President Grant signed a bill into law that placed a 3,350-square-mile parcel of wilderness under federal protection as "a public park and pleasuring ground for the benefit and enjoyment of the people." It was larger in size than the states of Delaware and Rhode Island put together.

Thus, Yellowstone became the first national park in the world. Today it is one of the largest and most popular of fifty-nine national parks in the United States and of over five hundred in seventy-two other nations. The national park concept just may have been America's greatest gift to humankind.

Of course Washburn and his associates were not the first humans in the Yellowstone wilderness. Anonymous explorers and hunters came and went without ceremony. The lost and all-but-forgotten Truman Everts, for example, was rescued by two wandering mountain men, names unknown. They came upon him, near death, not far from where he had been lost. His feet were badly frozen, and his hip had been burned when he fell into scalding water where he had crouched to keep warm. He was incoherent and emaciated from a diet of elk thistles and roots. His weight had fallen to about sev-enty-five pounds. As miraculous as Everts' rescue was his ultimate recovery.

For about eleven thousand years before the first Europeans arrived, parties of primitive hunters had roamed Yellowstone Country in search of game. The earliest of these sought such Ice Age giants as wooly mammoths and prehistoric bison. Later, Native Americans hunted deer, sheep, and elk in the same region. Yet there remains little evidence of their presence. Maybe they feared the area's geology, which seemed to be alive and always angry. The only people known to live year-round in Yellowstone were the Sheepeaters, withdrawn and unaggressive mountain-dwellers of Shoshone or Bannock origin who inhabited the interior of Yellowstone sometime before Columbus waded ashore in the New World. The Sheepeaters subsisted largely on the bighorn sheep they hunted. They were few in number, and the first non–Native American visitors (beaver trappers and itinerant mountain men) found them living peacefully, wearing sheepskins and using tools fashioned from ram's horns and elk antlers.

The identity of the first beaver trapper–wanderer to penetrate deep into Yellowstone is not known. Many arrived from the eastern United States to search for the rich brown pelts that were in great worldwide demand, though the Yellowstone wilderness may not have been as fertile a trapping ground for beavers as Jackson Hole to the south and other sites in the Rockies. Among the first trappers of reliable record was John Colter, a Virginian who spent three years with Lewis and Clark Expeditions before choosing in 1807 to remain in the West as a freelance trapper. Until the time of Colter's death, no one really believed his accounts of Yellowstone's steaming infernos and fountains. Even Colter is said to have doubted his own recollections late in life.

Nor did anyone believe Jim Bridger, whose stories were even more extravagant than Colter's. Bridger described such "impossibles" as transparent mountains, petrified animals in petrified burial grounds, and fishing holes (most likely on the Firehole River) where Bridger could hook a trout and turn around and boil it just a few feet away for lunch. Amazingly, that was—and is today—possible.

Joe Meek was another youthful trapper who told wild tales about his Yellowstone adventures. During the 1820s Meek was separated from his group of fellow trappers during a mid-winter skirmish with attack. He wan-

Trout Creek makes a nearly circular meander on its way to the Yellowstone River in Hayden Valley.

dered alone for days before rejoining his friends, who were ensconced in comfort and warmth beside a hot springs basin.

During the 1830s the beaver-trapping bonanza was petering out and Yellowstone visitors changed from trappers to young adventurers. Some were entrepreneurs. By 1834 Warren Ferris, a surveyor by trade, had heard the reports of Colter, Bridger, and Meek and may even have talked to one of them. He had to see the wonders of Yellowstone for himself. Ferris explored widely and with an open mind, rather than with a purely predatory eye, and confirmed most of what the trappers had already reported. Today national park historians regard Ferris as the first of the millions of tourists who would follow.

Another young man of the same ilk was Osborne Russell, originally from Maine. In 1835 Russell guided a hunting party into the park and was so impressed with the Lamar River valley that he dreamed of living the rest of his life there. The words in his journal about this "Secluded Valley" sound surprisingly like those of a modern travel writer who has just visited the place on assignment. Russell wrote that "happiness and contentment

seemed to reign there in wild romantic splendor surrounded by majestic battlements."

Still, another four or five decades passed before most Americans had even the haziest idea of what lie in Yellowstone country, or that a new national park existed there. No tangible proof—no photographs—had yet been made depicting the geysers and canyons, the mud volcanos and howling wolves. All they had were unsubstantiated words of restless, unreliable men too far away.

Without public knowledge and therefore without public concern, the first national park had an early history of neglect, exploitation, and little conservation. At one time or another the Yellowstone region had been claimed by England, France, Spain, and the United States; at that time no one remotely regarded the Native Americans as owners. Once the United States had firm control of the area, Yellowstone belonged successively to Louisiana, Missouri, Oregon, Washington, Nebraska, Dakota, and finally to Wyoming, with thin strips of the park extending into Idaho and Montana.

In 1881 N. P. (nicknamed National Park) Langford was named the first superintendent of Yellowstone

Grotto Geyser is only a short hike or cross-country ski tour from the lodgings at Old Faithful.

Park—a dubious honor, as he served for five years without pay. So did the next four superintendents following him. Congress enacted no laws to protect the park and appropriated no money to maintain it. Unrestricted hunting continued as before. Forest fires were set deliberately, sometimes to drive game, sometimes as deliberate acts of vandalism. The first tourists, whose stagecoaches were sometimes held up by outlaws, openly shot bison. Bears and elk were killed for their hides and teeth, and just as often for no reason at all. In time wolves would be eliminated from the park altogether.

Fortunately, wildlife is a renewable resource that, when protected, can recover, and in time most Yellowstone species did. But some damage to the environment in those early days was permanent and widespread. Tons of trash were dumped into hot springs. Bath houses were built and bathing pools excavated into limestone rock. An entire geyser cone was removed and shipped to Washington for exhibition at the Smithsonian Institution, where it soon disintegrated into dust. Another notable instance of destruction occurred in 1885 when a Chinese laundryman found that pouring lye or soap into geysers would make them erupt prematurely while tourists applauded. His discovery ruined, or at least altered, more than one thermal system forever.

Somehow the park survived and remained, some scientists agree, relatively intact. Among the reasons were its great size, its inaccessibility, its deep and frigid winters, and its short summers. Virtually all of the early visitors arrived by train, and for a long while the closest railroad passed through Salt Lake City, four hundred miles away. In time a rail line was built to Gardiner, Montana, at the park's north boundary, making the construction of several hotels feasible and profitable. Sadly, all of these were located much too near to the area's most prominent natural features. The Old Faithful Inn stands only about three hundred steps from Old Faithful Geyser. Lake Hotel is nearer than that to Yellowstone Lake. Other concessions were built on the very rim of the Grand Canyon of the Yellowstone River.

Another reason that Yellowstone survives intact today was the presence of the United States Army. In 1886 management of the park was handed over to the U.S. Cavalry, who protected the park until 1916 when Congress authorized a new National Park Service. Soldiers stationed at key points, patrolled vigorously and almost eliminated poaching and vandalism, built roads, and in

At daybreak a bison bull is mirrored in Trout Creek, a tributary of the Yellowstone River in Hayden Valley.

general reestablished law and order. One of the early military "superintendents" was Captain George Anderson, whose enthusiasm for the park and for his task was unlimited. He was an early, active conservationist and a member of the Boone and Crockett Club, an influential group organized by, among others, Theodore Roosevelt.

When Anderson arrived in Yellowstone the last of ten million American bison were making a final stand in the American wilderness there on the high plateau. And even there not many roamed free. They might have vanished altogether except for one of Anderson's men, U.S. Army scout Burgess. His story must be among the most dramatic in the annals of early Yellowstone.

At dawn one March day in 1896 or 1897 a savage late-winter storm swirled over the high Yellowstone Plateau. The temperature was close to zero and a wild wind raged. Burgess debated whether to hole up alone at cold and cavernous Lake Hotel until the storm passed or to continue what seemed a hopeless mission: to find and capture an elusive bison poacher. Burgess's left foot, from which Crow Indians had chopped the toes years before,

pained him terribly. Nevertheless, he decided to continue on.

Strapping "snowshoes" (skis cabin-crafted of twelve-foot lodgepole pine slivers) onto his boots and using a willow sapling as his single ski pole, Burgess headed eastward across the frozen outlet of Yellowstone Lake to follow Pelican Creek, also a solid sheet of ice. He had to travel rapidly to keep from freezing. Suddenly he stopped in disbelief. Just ahead were the fresh tracks of another man on crude skis. In that vast, uninhabited wilderness, Burgess knew the trail could only have been made by one person: Ed Howell, the poacher he was hunting. Orders were to capture the outlaw, preferably alive, but dead if necessary. Burgess hesitated before he turned to follow the track which was quickly filling with wind-driven snow.

Even today, with the finest modern equipment, cross-country skiers do not attempt to traverse the Yellowstone Plateau without great preparations and apprehension. But Ed Howell was no ordinary man. In fact, if Howell had been anything but a poacher and an outlaw, he might today be regarded with Jim Bridger, John Colter, and Jedediah Smith among the greatest outdoorsmen and frontier heroes. Built like a grizzly, tough and tenacious almost beyond description, he was a master at survival. Earlier that winter on slat skis he had carved out with his axe, he had pulled a toboggan loaded with 180 pounds of supplies from Cooke City to Pelican Creek—a trip of about forty miles as a raven flies, but several times that distance on foot over treacherous mountain terrain.

Howell didn't even own a good pair of boots; he wrapped his feet in gunny sacking and then stepped into "meal sack" bindings nailed to twelve-foot skis. A cur dog was his only companion. It is entirely possible that Howell was the inventor of step (no-wax) skis that became popular almost a century later. He used an axe to make cut marks across his ski base to give a better grip when climbing a slope and used pine tree resin to prevent snow from sticking.

Howell pitched a tepee at Astringent Creek (Pelican Meadow) and from that rude base began shooting the buffalo that were wintering thereabouts. At that time *all* (a few hundred) of the park's bison wintered there. Shooting them was often very easy because the bison were trapped in basins surrounded by deep snow. Howell would cache their hides and heads (in great demand by eastern taxidermists) deep in the lodgepole pine forests and out of reach of roaming wolf packs, for collection in spring. He did not believe that anyone could find, or would even look for, his isolated hunting camp. It was the last and maybe the only mistake Howell ever made.

Traveling as rapidly as possible upwind in the storm, scout Burgess followed the ski tracks to Howell's tepee, where several fresh bison robes were hanging. Pausing there, he heard six faraway shots fired at intervals. Burgess moved off in the direction of the shots, skiing very slowly now, his heart pounding—but not from the exertion alone. Soon he came to an open white meadow stained red. About four hundred yards away a man was bending down to skin one of five dead buffalo that littered the landscape. Howell's rifle was leaning against a carcass about fifteen feet away, but still within easy reach.

Armed only with a .38 service revolver, Burgess had to make a perfect stalk or be killed. Fortunately the sound of the wind blowing harder by the minute muffled the noise of his approach. He crept unnoticed to within ten feet of the poacher, who was elbow deep in blood and gore.

"Drop the knife," Burgess said. To this day that knife may lie where it fell at that moment.

Burgess marched his prisoner first to Lake for the night (he had already skied over eighteen miles since daybreak) and then northward toward Old Faithful, where he turned Howell over to the detachment of troops in the area. According to Emerson Hough, a writer for the then-influential *Forest & Stream* magazine in New York (and who visited Yellowstone the next spring), Howell was unrepentant and ate twenty-eight pancakes for his first meal in captivity. Nothing is known of his fate thereafter. He was never heard from again.

Burgess's capture of Howell may have saved the buffalo in Yellowstone Park and elsewhere; today they thrive in increasing to almost unmanageable numbers. Visitors to Yellowstone now encounter them more often than any other species of wildlife. But Burgess did not fare so well; the Army post surgeon had to amputate the badly frost-bitten toes on the foot that the Crows had spared years before. Despite the importance of his accomplishments, Burgess's first name, his origin, and everything else about the man remains a mystery to this day. But we all are greatly in his debt.

Inevitably Yellowstone became a magnet for anyone with a spirit of adventure, especially for those who could afford to travel the long distances to reach it. They came for various reasons. Reportedly, the first man to climb Grand Teton peak, just south of Yellowstone, also became the first to cross the park on a bicycle in 1883. W. O. Owen and other members of the Laramie (Wyoming) Bicycle Club accomplished this on bikes with huge, five-foot-diameter front wheels and tiny back ones, then in vogue. Biking in the park never did catch on, at first because of the horrible roads and later because of hazardous competition with automobiles.

Two years later, during the very rainy summer of 1885, one of America's greatest advocates of wilderness arrived in the park. Despite a nagging illness and a fall from his horse on a narrow trail, John Muir was completely enchanted with the lonely land he explored. In fact, Muir's most famous quotation was written about Yellowstone, not about Yosemite as is commonly believed. He wrote, "Climb the mountains and get their good tidings. Nature's peace will flow into you as sunshine flows into trees. The winds will blow their freshness into you and the storms their energy, while cares will drop off like autumn leaves."

Steam rises hundreds of feet above Old Faithful Geyser, here in the final phase of eruption.

Red Wyoming, or Indian Paintbrush, is a common summer wildflower on mountain slopes and in meadows. Peak blooming is in July.

Muir also made a suggestion in his Yellowstone essay that would make park rangers shudder today. "Climb Electric Peak," he wrote, "when a big, bossy well-charged thundercloud is on it, to breathe the ozone set free, and get yourself kindly shaken and shocked. You are sure to be lost in wonder and praise, and every hair on your head will stand up and hum and sing like an enthusiastic congregation."

Rudyard Kipling passed through Yellowstone at the turn of the century and, unlike Muir and most others, did not enjoy himself. Pausing en route from India to England, he seemed more interested in why some people spit and in running over a skunk in the dark than in the stunning beauty on every side. "Today I am in the Yellowstone Park," the man wrote about his stagecoach ride to Mammoth Hot Springs, "and I wish I were dead." Kipling went on to refer to the Norris Geyser Basin as "the uplands of Hell," and noted that the mud volcanos "spat filth into Heaven."

Civil War union generals Sherman and Sheridan both visited the park. So did the famous 240-pound New York painter and sculptor Frederic Remington. He was impressed by almost everything he saw, especially the grizzly bears and the abundance of waterfowl. "Nature had made her wildest patterns here," Remington concluded.

Teddy Roosevelt's first journey to the park in the 1880s had much to do with his great interests in nature, outdoor recreation, and conservation. But better known is his sentimental visit in 1903 as part of a grand western tour that also included Yosemite. Unlike the entourage of President Chester Arthur (who arrived with a battalion of dignitaries and an elegant, almost royal camp), Roosevelt toured with a small staff that included naturalist/writer John Burroughs. En route from Gardiner to Mammoth one day, the two counted hundreds of "prongbuck" (pronghorns or antelope) and large herds of elk, exactly as a traveler might encounter in the same sector today.

Other American presidents followed Roosevelt's footsteps to Yellowstone, but he probably was the last one to come without some political or popularity motive, trailed by cameramen. Calvin Coolidge came in 1926 and went fishing a few times without enthusiasm, his stiff collar

This bull elk is one of hundreds of large animals that will spend winter in the foothills zone around Gardiner and the park's north entrance.

After the August rut, antelope rest on a warm autumn day near Stephens Creek at the park's north boundary.

and tie securely around his neck. Meanwhile, Grace Coolidge organized dances for the younger guests at Mammoth Hotel. Gerald Ford worked one summer as a temporary park employee, just as I did, but apparently he was less affected by it. (If I were ever elected president, my conservation record would be a lot better than his.)

There simply is no place on earth to match Yellowstone Park, and it is no wonder that annually the flood of tourists increases. It is a premier, natural, international attraction. What was a trickle of tourists at the beginning of the twentieth century grew sharply just after World War II, most arriving by family car driven on newly improved transcontinental highways. Since 1965 two million or more travelers have passed through Yellowstone each year, with at least 90 percent arriving between June and August. As I write this in 1992, about forty thousand people enjoy the park on any summer day. There is plenty to interest and enthrall them, even if they stay all summer.

Overleaf: A late-summer sun sets over the Madison River. Smoke from forest fires outside the park provide an eerie glow.

A herd of bison in Hayden Valley ford Alum Creek, which is swollen by springtime rains and runoff.

THE YELLOWSTONE LANDSCAPE

There are two distinctly different Yellowstones. Best known is the one easily visible from park roads. The other is found beyond the blacktop, by trail, usually just a short distance beyond the trailhead. But the serenity and stillness you find off the highways could change suddenly. This land is a product of one of the most violent eras of volcanism known to geologic science, and earthquakes still occur with some frequency. The blasts and upheavals that once tortured this high plateau, which rises from a mile to more than two miles above sea level, were so cataclysmic that it is impossible to comprehend or describe them. Today hikers can see evidence of this violence almost everywhere they walk.

All of Yellowstone was once submerged under a great, shallow inland sea. During a first upheaval, about two million years ago, hundreds of cubic miles of ash and pumice exploded out of the earth's core in just a short time, raising the land out of the sea. A million years later there were more explosions. Finally, 600,000 years ago, there was a third round that was a thousand times more powerful than the eruption of Mount St. Helens, Washington, in 1980. This one cracked and collapsed the earth's crust. When the turmoil subsided, much of Yellowstone as we find it now had been created.

Modern geologists believe that the final upheaval probably began with an upsurge of magma (underground molten rock) great enough to form a mountain about sixty miles in diameter. Unable to contain the material swelling up from below, the mountain fractured and be-

gan a massive eruption. It has been described as a geologic holocaust of rumbling, flying pumice, lava flows, debris, and exploding gas, perhaps the most violent convulsion ever on this planet. Ash was blown fifty miles high, and ash deposits were enough to form Mount Washburn and other park peaks.

What Yellowstone visitors find now is a volcanic landscape that long ago cooled and solidified. It is striking and beautiful to see—even frightening to some. Weathering and erosion over centuries have softened the landscape, and vegetation has covered much of it, but in places the patterns of ancient lava flows still exist underfoot. Lower temperatures and the age of glaciers carved Yellowstone's valleys and canyons into the stark forms we know and photograph in the park today.

Walk along the popular trails or boardwalks and you may have a mildly uneasy feeling. The geysers and hot springs, the fumaroles, the steaming pools and belching mud pots, even a ground much warmer than the atmosphere: All are signs that magma still exists down there only a mile or two below the surface. (Elsewhere in North America, the hot magma rests forty or more miles below the surface.) Cold groundwaters from winter's heavy snowpack trickle down through fissures, faults, and porous rock toward the magma. It may take sixty years or more before water and magma meet. But at such depths the water may be heated to over six hundred degrees Fahrenheit and still be liquid, at a pressure of about 2,400 pounds per square inch. Eventually, per-

Even with winter temperatures falling far below zero, thermal waters prevent the Firehole River from freezing over.

Bison cross a slough of the Yellowstone River in Hayden Valley. A large part of the park's bison herd live in or within reach of this valley.

haps after centuries underground, the water boils back upward through subterranean caverns, or "pipes." It then escapes as the steam jet of a geyser or, not erupting, as the scalding hot water that flows over delicate terraces, as at Mammoth Hot Springs.

Consider a few interesting figures. At sea level water boils at 212 degrees Fahrenheit, but at Yellowstone altitudes it boils at less than 200 degrees. The coffee you sip around a Yellowstone campfire is probably between 130 and 140 degrees, noticeably cooler than most are accustomed to. A shower at Old Faithful Hotel is too hot if it exceeds 110 degrees. But throughout the park there are bacteria that live in water that is boiling. Some of the colors you find in the thermal areas are mineral deposits, as from sulphur or iron oxides. But more of that color comes from living organisms, perhaps from certain blue-green algae that manage to live in water that's 165 degrees Fahrenheit.

Thus, strange as it may seem, a chain of life in Yellowstone begins in the flowing thermal waters. All of the multicolored algae produce chlorophyll that uses the radiant energy of sunlight to transform inorganic material into microscopic food. A number of different flies,

also tolerant of heat, eat the food and are in turn eaten by larger insects and by such birds as the killdeer. Anything not eaten dies and is recycled, decomposed by bacteria.

During the 1970s researcher Thomas Brock discovered a heat-tolerant bacteria new to science. He named it *Sulfolobus acidocaldarius*. This unique organism lives, among other places, beside Gibbon Meadow, a grazing area for elk herds at Evening Primrose Spring. The water temperature here is often as high as 195 degrees Fahrenheit, too hot for all but a few *Sulfolobus* to survive. The churning surface of the spring is covered with a thick, yellow, frothy sulphur mat. Whenever the water temperature falls to 167 degrees Fahrenheit or so, ideal for growth and survival of bacteria, the *Sulfolobus* eat all the sulphur. This results in a spring of sulphuric acid (and Yellowstone's most acidic spring), strong enough to dissolve cotton or woolen clothing.

Around many thermal areas a smell like rotten eggs is pervasive, unpleasant to many. This odor comes from the bacteria-produced sulphuric acid and from the oxidation of hydrogen sulphide gas bubbling to the surface. Most mud pots bubbling and belching around the park are really hot, acidic clay soups.

Mud pots can grow quite large and loud, occasionally sounding like an artillery brigade firing salvos in the distance. In 1870 members of the Washburn Expedition detoured a half mile from their planned course to find a violent mud "volcano" that had splattered lodgepole pines 150 feet away with blobs of mud. More than a century later this same thermal feature had "traveled" about three-quarters of a mile westward. It was belching huge balls of mud as far as two hundred feet away. But by late 1980 it had all but dried up. This mud pot's demise may have been caused by frequent small earthquakes during the previous two years.

During the winter many hydrothermal areas serve as oases of warmth in a bitterly cold world. The vegetation around hot springs and geysers is normally very sparse because of the numbers of large animals, especially elk and bison, that crowd around them during intense cold periods. Likewise, any streams or ponds kept ice-free by the flow of warm water are precious wintering and feeding areas for waterfowl. Peggy and I have even found yellow and dwarf monkeyflowers blooming beside a rivulet of warm water just inches from crusty snow. The thermal areas regulate the number of individual animals of various wildlife species that can live year-round in Yellowstone Park.

There are important geothermal areas elsewhere in the world, but none match those in Yellowstone. Those in Iceland and on New Zealand's North Island, which we have visited, have been exploited for power and other commercial purposes, with dire consequences. Iceland's geothermals have been all but destroyed; only fourteen of New Zealand's original 130 geysers still erupt today. So far the thermal areas at the Krontoski Biological Reserve in Siberia remain intact.

In a 1988 survey, it was estimated that Yellowstone contained about ten thousand thermal features, ranging from tiny sylvan rivulets to entire mountainsides that roar. This estimate included all the known active boiling pools and cauldrons, the mud pots and sulphur vents, the steaming grottos and geysers, and the exquisite travertine springs. But that total may have been flawed, because familiar thermals sometimes vanish while new ones appear or are discovered for the first time. Thermal activity might certainly have been greater in Jim Bridger's or Teddy Roosevelt's day than it will be next summer. Furthermore, the intensity of an active thermal area may vary from year to year. As yet there is no foolproof way to explain the variances or to make predictions.

Excelsior Geyser is an excellent example of such unpredictability. Once the most powerful geyser in the park, periodically erupting over three hundred feet into the thin atmosphere, Excelsior suddenly stopped erupting in 1888. Since then it has been a major hot spring, daily discharging about five million gallons of scalding water into the Firehole River. But do not be surprised if without warning it starts to erupt again. Other geysers have done so.

Old Faithful surely deserves to be thought of as the symbol and spirit of Yellowstone. A few of the park's three hundred geysers are larger, but to me few spectacles are as awesome as this huge, steaming fountain shooting upward between one hundred and two hundred feet into the sky. On winter days when the temperature is below freezing, bright Old Faithful seems to rise twice that high, but it is an optical illusion.

During the two-to-five-minute duration of an eruption, Old Faithful spews about 8,400 gallons of water and about sixty-five pounds of dissolved silica from its ground vent, or opening. It is a tremendously powerful sight. The jet begins as a waist-high column of water and steam. Then the sound of rushing air, water, and steam increases in volume as another and yet another plume pulses upward, higher and ever higher. Then, when it seems it couldn't reach any closer to the clouds, the geyser makes a last enormous effort and outdoes everything that came before. Finally with a sigh the last of the vapor evaporates and the last droplets disappear back down the vent.

Despite its name, Old Faithful is not entirely faithful. With a camera mounted on a tripod we have waited as little as thirty-five minutes for the eruption and as long as an hour and a half. But the average interval between performances over the past several years has been seventy-seven minutes. By timing an eruption with a stopwatch while estimating the volume of water expelled, park rangers have a formula by which they can predict the time, within five to ten minutes, of the next eruption. A sign is posted with this calculation for the convenience of visitors.

During an early visit to Yellowstone I enjoyed a surprising encounter with a geyser more dependable than Old Faithful. Early one August morning, while flycasting in the Firehole River, I felt the earth tremble underfoot,

The mood at Mammoth Hot Springs terraces changes constantly under Montana's big and threatening sky.

and an instant later Riverside Geyser sent a plume of steaming water completely over my fishing hole. Never before had I been sprayed in such a beautiful setting. The oblique, arching eruption lasted for about twenty minutes, as they always have, erupting every six and a half hours or so.

Generally, the most memorable geysers are also those that are easiest to see because, in the early days of the park, roads were surveyed to make them most accessible. Many experts consider Castle Geyser the oldest in the park. Its cone is about 125 feet in girth and is still "growing," or building up. Its eruptions of water followed by a steam jet last for about an hour.

Beehive Geyser is one of several with a strange shape of cone that has solidified around the vent. Not at all predictable, Beehive shoots a powerful stream of water through a small nozzle in its beehive-shaped cone about 150 feet high.

We often see Grotto Geyser erupting; it does so about fifty percent of the time. The steaming water rarely shoots out higher than ten feet, but the cone is fantastic enough in shape to make it an unusual sight. Among my most memorable moments in Yellowstone was a cold March morning when Peggy and I went exploring on skis across Upper Geyser Basin. The fog and mist were so thick that we came upon a ghostly, scattered elk band and small flocks of Canada geese (which flushed noisily) almost before we could see them. Suddenly we also came upon Grotto Geyser, the sound of its ongoing eruption almost completely muffled. I will never forget that eerie experience.

Unlike Grotto, whose strange cone gradually built up around skeletons of trees that grew on the spot, some geysers, called fountain geysers, have no cones. Among the most amazing of these is Great Fountain. Its vent is covered by a pool of hot water, and about three times during each twenty-four-hour period it erupts to a height of about two hundred feet.

Geysers may be the most spectacular of the hydrothermals, depending on your preference, but some other thermals may be more beautiful. It is difficult not to single out the Mammoth Hot Springs area, where many of the terraces resemble caves turned inside out. Terraces here and elsewhere are created when water, which in this case is really a hot carbonic acid solution, seeks the surface, where it cools. The dissolved carbon dioxide is precipitated out as mineral travertine deposits.

These deposits—as much as two tons added every day in the Mammoth area—cause the terraces to grow . . . and grow.

As if the geothermal activity doesn't furnish enough excitement, Yellowstone ranks among the most likely places on the North American continent to experience an earthquake. Seismographs, which monitor the park lands, record about thirty tremors every year. Most are scarcely noticeable. But just at dusk on August 17, 1959, an earthquake measuring a powerful 7.1 on the Richter scale began. With its epicenter just outside Yellowstone Park, this one was felt across eight western states and throughout western Canada. Twenty-eight people perished under rock slides in Madison Canyon just west of Yellowstone. Quake Lake, seventeen miles northwest of the town of West Yellowstone, was formed when waters were impounded by a dam composed of the debris of massive landslides carrying an estimated forty-three million cubic yards of rock.

Few visitors in the park that night will ever forget stumbling out of their hotels in pajamas and nightgowns into total darkness. The ancient chimney at Old Faithful buckled and cracked, but remained intact. A newly installed fire sprinkler system split, dousing some of the escapees with a cold shower on their way out. Some small buildings at both Mammoth and Old Faithful were rendered useless and one or two collapsed. Yellowstone's loop road was blocked by rock slides in three places: Firehole Canyon, Gibbon Falls, and Virginia Cascades. At sunrise the earth was quiet, but Yellowstone was drained of many of its summer guests.

The 1959 earthquake gave geothermal scientists something to think about. Soon after the main shock, about three hundred geysers erupted. Half of these had not been known to erupt before. In the following days other thermal activities were altered. At Biscuit Basin, for instance, placid Sapphire Pool blew out fifty- to one-hundred-pound chunks of earth in violent eruptions. Yellowstone's underground "plumbing" had apparently been altered, plugging up some of the "pipes" (vents) and creating new pressures and vents at the surface.

Although it seems logical that no sensible person or society would ever want to meddle with the precious natural phenomena of Yellowstone, the opposite is true. From time to time, schemes have been proposed by politicians and entrepreneurs to tap the thermal "wealth" and use it "for the good of man." As recently as 1992 Director Dallas Peck of the U.S. Geological Survey stated in a report that "some use of Yellowstone's geothermal water could be made with no discernible risk." It was a most irresponsible opinion.

The Church Universal and Triumphant, a religious sect, owns a large ranch adjoining Yellowstone Park, just six miles north of Mammoth Hot Springs. In 1986 the church tapped into LaDuke Hot Springs on its own property. Soon after, LaDuke dried up, sending a signal to Yellowstone Park officials to stop further tampering, since the entire system is interconnected.

What better use for the thermal areas could there possibly be than "for the benefit and enjoyment of the people," as stated in the charter President Grant signed in 1872?

A small geyser in the Upper Geyser Basin boils and percolates before overflowing into the Firehole River just behind.

An eruption of Castle Geyser blots out the sun, and the spray covers a wide area of the Geyser Basin.

Dwarf monkeyflowers at Upper Geyser Basin are among the earliest flowers to bloom in the park.

Grand Canyon rim trails near Canyon lead to overlooks offering spectacular views such as this one of the Yellowstone River below Lower Falls.

Above left: *A short hike from the Gibbon River and Elk Meadow leads to Fountain Paint Pots, an especially colorful cluster of boiling hot springs.* **Above right:** *It's been estimated that Yellowstone contains about ten thousand thermal features, including boiling pots and cauldrons, mud pots, sulphur vents, geysers, and travertine springs. Here, steam at Midway Geyser Basin lends a mystical quality to the Yellowstone landscape.* **Left:** *Castle Geyser, here beginning to erupt, was named by members of the 1870 Washburn Expedition because it then resembled "a striking castle or tower."*

In early autumn, rabbitbrush blooms beside a roadside pond near Junction Butte.

Mineral-laden hot water from far underground cascades over the main terrace at Mammoth Hot Springs. Unaccountably, the water flow increases and decreases from year to year.

Deep in the Grand Canyon, the Yellowstone River plunges 308 feet over Lower Falls. The sight and sound of the falls are breathtaking from overlooks along the Grand Canyon's edge.

THE WILDLIFE OF YELLOWSTONE

Soon after daybreak one unforgettable morning in June 1991, Peggy and I came upon a spectacle that might only have been matched on the Kenya or Tanzania plains in East Africa. Driving southward from Canyon Village we noticed that heavy spring runoffs had raised and roiled the Yellowstone River. In fact, the river had flooded much of the meadow of Alum Creek, a tributary, and in that meadow was a bewildering concentration of wildlife that we may never see again.

A herd of a hundred or so bison were drinking and grazing in the new green grass around the fringe of the flooded area. A cow moose with a week-old calf also grazed, keeping a discreet distance from the bison. Between the two in deeper water a phalanx of a dozen white pelicans were fishing in their unique coordinated style. Everywhere were waterfowl, some feeding, some preening, others courting: Canada geese, mallards, American widgeon, pintails, Barrow's goldeneyes, green-winged teal, common mergansers, and others, everywhere on the surface of the shallow water. Many California gulls and a few common terns circled above the ducks.

As we hurried to set up cameras on tripods between the road and water's edge, I also counted sandhill cranes, a cowbird riding on a bison's back, a pair of savannah sparrows in the roadside brush, several Wilson's phalaropes, and a spotted sandpiper not far away. It is no wonder I developed ten thumbs on my two hands as I tried to focus a camera on some part of that remarkable scene. Believe it or not, that is when a weasel suddenly appeared on my left, ran right over my boots, and vanished in the vegetation on my right. Only in Yellowstone Park could all this happen in a few minutes.

From time to time Montana and Wyoming travel commissions have surveyed Yellowstone travelers. When asked what they enjoyed most in the park, visitors invariably said it was the wildlife. In fact, Yellowstone's flora and fauna have always appealed to far more visitors than even the area's geothermal features. For me that is easy to understand. Nothing is more fascinating than living wild creatures in Yellowstone—or anywhere, for that matter. And nothing is more addicting than photographing them.

One of the first biologists to explore Yellowstone was C. Hart Merriam, who visited during the 1890s. As he climbed the mountains he noted dramatic changes in environment and saw that the type of habitat altered with elevation. Thus Merriam conceived his theory of life zones. Each zone, with its distinctive moisture levels, temperature variations, and vegetation, supports its own community of wildlife. While most animals do not venture from their own area, some range seasonally through several zones. At one time or another bighorn sheep and elk are found in all of them.

Lowest in elevation of Yellowstone's life zones, though still considerably higher than what most of us are accustomed to, is the foothills zone. This area lies between five thousand and six thousand feet above sea level, about a mile high. It is located in the north-central part of the park, and consists of mainly open, dry, heavily grazed (in winter) grassland with sagebrush and some cottonwood and juniper trees.

The foothills merge into the montane zone (6,000–7,600 feet), a combination of forested and open habitat. Douglas firs are the dominant trees in this zone, accompanied by quaking aspens, Engelmann spruce,

At daybreak in mid-September, a bull elk pauses beside the Madison River. A harem of cows is hidden in shadows across the river.

subalpine fir, and a few lodgepole pines. Lodgepoles become the dominant trees in the subalpine zone (7,600–10,000 feet) and are by far the most abundant trees in the park.

The highest of Yellowstone's life zones is the alpine zone, ranging from 10,000 feet to the park's highest point, Eagle Peak, at 11,538 feet. The alpine zone is a treeless area above timberline. It is tundra and meltwater meadows mixed with rock fields on which short grasses, sedges, and hardy wildflowers grow in summer. High winds blow here, and day in and day out the temperatures in the alpine zone average fifteen degrees Fahrenheit lower than those in the foothills zone.

In all four Yellowstone life zones only about 1,200 different plants have been cataloged. By contrast, twice that many might grow on a single acre of undisturbed Amazon rainforest. Nor by comparison are the numbers of species of mammals (58) or birds (252) living in Yellowstone very great. But the tremendous advantage here is that everyone can watch and enjoy the wildlife the year around.

One mammal we did not see at Alum Creek that incredible day in 1991, but which usually was visible there in years past, was the finest symbol of the Yellowstone wilderness, the grizzly bear (also called the brown bear). We seem to spot fewer and fewer of them each summer and have the uneasy feeling that they are not doing well, not prospering as they should. Most authorities estimate the number of grizzlies living today in the Greater Yellowstone Ecosystem at between 180 and 200.

When discussing grizzlies and Yellowstone it is impossible not to recall the wildlife biologists and twin brothers Frank and John Craighead, who began a comprehensive study of the species there in 1959, where (and when) the largest number of grizzly bears still survived south of Canada. Neither grizzlies nor any other wildlife would be so thoroughly examined scientifically in the park during the next seven years.

The Craigheads knew they would need radically new techniques to study an elusive wild mammal that might daily roam from horizon to horizon over the roughest terrain and then hibernate for half a year beneath a remote snowbound windfall or in a cave. The brothers thus became the first to develop and use a then-new space science called biotelemetry. By live-capturing grizzlies, tranquilizing them, and affixing radio trans-

mitters, the Craigheads were able to pry into their private lives from a distance. Heretofore most "knowledge" of grizzlies had come from cattle ranchers or hunters studying the animals over gunsights. The Craighead project officially began on June 26, 1959, when the gate of their baited culvert trap slammed shut on an angry bruin.

During the next year the researchers, along with student assistants and myself once or twice, captured and marked with ear tags thirty more grizzlies. Some were lured into the standard culvert traps; others were taken with drug-filled darts shot into their rumps at close range. It was a most exciting life during which the Craigheads followed on foot, and virtually lived with, certain grizzlies for long periods of time. Obviously it would be impossible to handle 391 different bears a total of six hundred times in seven years without a traumatic experience or two. There was the day, for example, when one heavy male nicknamed Ivan the Terrible recovered too quickly from the tranquilizer and exploded into action. After smashing their scales and medical kit, Ivan chased the brothers into their station wagon, slammed into the closing door, and then tried to claw its way through the windshield.

I like to think that the grizzlies we see today in the distance on Mount Washburn and along Pebble Creek are individuals like some of those I saw while observing the Craigheads. Pegleg, for instance, really didn't need an ear tag because he could be identified by his unique, stiff-legged walk. The lower lip of Cutlip hung askew, perhaps having been torn in a fight. Sucostrin Kid needed more than the dose of tranquilizer that would usually immobilize an animal of his size. Loverboy had a scar under one eye and was missing part of an ear. Owl Face reminded Frank Craighead of a short-eared owl, but is best remembered as the first grizzly sow ever confirmed to have adopted the cubs of another female. One year another character, Grizzled Sow, produced an unusually large litter of four cubs, which she commanded with almost military discipline.

Early in October 1986 Peggy and I were photographing the rutting activities of elk when word circulated through Norris Campground, where we were based, that a photographer was missing. Three days later park rangers found the body of William Tesinsky as a female grizzly was trying to drag it away. They shot the bear. Nearby they found Tesinsky's bent tripod and cam-

Pine martens are not often seen, but they aren't shy and may be suddenly encountered along woodland trails or around old buildings.

era, caked with dried blood. Attached to the camera was an 80–200mm lens. A zoom lens of that focal length is too short for shooting potentially dangerous animals.

Guessing that the film in the camera might give some clue to what had happened, whether Tesinsky was taken by surprise or had approached too near the animal, park officials sent the roll to be developed. But it contained only two exposures of bison taken elsewhere and a final shot of an indistinct dark object, out of focus. Was it the attacking bear? A statement was later issued saying that Tesinsky had indeed been trying to photograph the killer. True or not, approaching a bear on foot anywhere in the park is bad business. Any time.

The plain truth, though, is that grizzly bear incidents in Yellowstone have been few since tourists began to arrive. An individual is far more likely to be killed or injured by lightning, drowning, car accident, domestic argument, even by a bee sting than by a bear. Of course, all precautions about bears issued by park officials should absolutely be observed. But I am convinced that Yellowstone bison, as lethargic as they sometimes seem, are vastly more dangerous than the bears.

One of the great changes in Yellowstone during my lifetime has been in the number of black bears that are visible there. Before the early 1970s, a visitor could not drive across the park without meeting and being delayed by a dozen or more bears panhandling along the main roads. I was always thrilled by the sight of them, but I realize it was not a good thing either for the bears (who came to depend on the human handouts) or for the tourists (who were compromising their own safety). Unfortunately, there was no solution other than to relocate many of the animals into remote park areas and to eliminate any that returned repeatedly. Some transplanted black bears had remarkable homing instincts. Carried as far as eighty miles away by truck or helicopter, beyond park borders, within a few days they were back patrolling their regular "beats" along the roadsides.

I have had my share of meetings with black bears, even with females with small cubs, without confrontation. When hiking on the trails Peggy and I always watch ahead for them and we give any we see plenty of room. Keeping your distance is especially important when the aroma of a dead animal, possibly a bear kill or cache, hangs in the air. All bears vigorously defend their food.

I recall just one time when it was possible to ignore the usual warnings. Early one fall a mule deer was struck by a car on the road in Gardner Canyon between Gardiner and Mammoth. Peggy and I drove along there just after a black bear had dragged the deer carcass across the Gardner River and had begun to dine on it on the far bank. Autumn is always a peak time for photographers in Yellowstone, and within an hour or two many were standing shoulder to shoulder with telephoto lenses focused on the bear, separated from the creature by a cold, swift current.

The show lasted for more than two days as the bruin alternately gorged and then slept right on top of its prize, until only the skeleton of the deer remained. Occasionally the bear would rouse itself long enough to scatter the magpies or ravens that tried to share in the bounty. Black bears relish meat, fresh or carrion, and will go to any extremes to obtain it, but they thrive in the Yellowstone wilderness because they are not selective. A black bear's diet is limited to anything that is edible.

Another carnivore, almost never seen, may be more numerous and widespread than believed until the 1990s. Recent investigations have shown that there is a significant population of mountain lions, or cougars, in the park. Only once have I seen a cougar in the Yellowstone area, in the Teton Wilderness just southeast of the park. But we have found cougar tracks in the northern sector where there are large numbers of elk and other ungulates year around, especially in winter. These handsome, tawny cats are the shyest of all the large mammals in America.

Not nearly so shy is another, smaller predator that has appeared frequently in my Yellowstone experiences—the coyote. Because hunting is illegal within park boundaries, coyotes are a lot less wary in Yellowstone than they are outside the park, where humans have used every conceivable means from poisons and high-powered rifles to electronics to get rid of them. Unlike their larger cousins, wolves, coyotes have survived and even flourished in the park. In fact, after all human and animal life has vanished from the face of the earth, coyotes may still roam the plains and woodlands.

A winter-killed animal carcass doesn't last very long before a coyote finds it. Their ability to locate carrion seems almost miraculous. During one particularly bitter January we saw a solitary coyote plowing through the shoulder-deep snow, apparently heading nowhere. For a long while through binoculars, from the Lamar Valley–Northeast Entrance Road, we watched this ani-

In midsummer, when the Yellowstone River level is low and aquatic vegetation lush, moose often graze in midstream.

White pelicans preen after fishing in the Yellowstone River. There is a pelican rookery on an island in southern Yellowstone Lake.

In a meadow near Mammoth, a cow elk licks her hours-old calf. Most elk calves are dropped in June.

mal travel in one direction, often barely able to make headway through the deep snow. Then late in the afternoon we discovered its destination: a winter-killed buffalo almost hidden in a snow drift. The only way it could possibly have located that carcass, more than three miles away, was by watching the flight of ravens that had found it first, knowing what such a grouping indicated, and making its way to the spot.

The next day our coyote, along with three others, was enjoying its bonanza, which probably lasted the trio a week or two. They paid little attention when I approached near enough to take pictures.

Many nights camping in Yellowstone have been more memorable because of coyotes singing beyond the tent, often quite close by. This howling is not perfectly understood, but Franz Camenzind, who studied the species at the National Elk Refuge south of the park, told me that the night yipping and barking of a group near a campsite was probably a declaration of family ties rather than just baying at the moon. Whatever the reason, they certainly sound like they are enjoying themselves.

Years ago a lone coyote enriched an otherwise ordinary trout fishing trip. I had hiked up Nez Perce Creek and, after casting for an hour or so without a rise, I sat down against a streambank to munch a sandwich. Halfway through it I had that eerie feeling of being watched. And I was. Across the creek a coyote sat upright, watching me, almost like an obedient dog waiting for its meal. Until it silently slipped away, I felt both foolish and guilty in not being able to share my lunch.

If you travel the park leisurely, even aimlessly, rather than rushing through as too many tourists do, the rewards can be tremendous. You'll see twice as many creatures as when pushing the speed limit on the roads. Early in the morning around the Grand Canyon rim that flash of red is a red fox. Pine martens are seen darting through any forest, and otters swim in all the larger waterways and are not especially wary here. A colony of yellow-bellied marmots lives in the Sheepeater Cliffs, and every campground is populated by red squirrels, golden-mantled or Uinta ground squirrels, chipmunks, or some combination of these. All are most appealing natives.

One animal encountered everywhere in Yellowstone is the American elk or wapiti, second in size only to the moose (also a Yellowstone resident) among all the world's deer. In 1992 an estimated eighteen thousand to twenty thousand elk inhabited the park—a number that may be beyond the carrying capacity of the range. You meet them on the green lawns near park headquarters and in the public campground at Mammoth. You find them along the roads, wading the rivers, and on backcountry trails. For any student of nature, wildlife, and wilderness, it is worth traveling halfway around the world just to see the spectacular elk rut of early autumn.

The elk's annual breeding season begins in early September, when the park is at its most beautiful, and we save a week or so to spend there each year at this time. The aspens have turned bright yellow, the air is crisp, and beneath morning frosts the grassy meadows are golden. In addition, most summer tourists have departed, the hotels are closing down, and the most serious nature lovers have the place all to themselves. Nowhere else on earth can the shrill, calliope bugling of testy, lovesick bull elk, down from the high country, be heard so clearly.

We set up camp at Mammoth or Madison or Norris, all of which are very near and sometimes even within sight of the rutting activities. That is important, because during the peak of the breeding period activity begins well before dawn.

One morning when camped at Norris, I was awakened by splashing in the Gibbon River nearby, and a moment later a bull elk bugled a challenge that must have been audible a mile away. Sitting upright in my sleeping bag, my breath white and heavy in the cold air, I pulled on two pairs of heavy woolen socks and shoved my feet into damp hip boots. As I put a pot of coffee to boil on a propane camp stove, I heard two bulls bugling back and forth. After wolfing down cold cereal along with the coffee, Peggy and I headed out single-mindedly toward the bugling with tripods and cameras over our shoulders.

We were so intent at first on finding the elk that we did not notice the fresh animal trail through the frosted, brittle, knee-high grass. But suddenly, from the width of it, I realized that a grizzly had passed by here only minutes earlier. The realization added a new dimension to our photography: Now we were watching for a bear as well as for the rutting elk. Soon the job was made easier by the weak sun that, blinking through lodgepole pines, gradually illuminated our side of the meadow.

The elk, yellow in the low light, stood about a hundred yards beyond the Gibbon River. The cows were grazing, heads down. In the center of this harem stood a splendid dark bull with fourteen ivory antler tips clearly

visible. Tilting the antlers back far enough to scrape its rump, while staring toward the sky, the bull whistled once more just as we waded into the stream. I have heard that challenge a hundred times before, but it never fails to raise the little hairs on the back of my neck.

Carefully, indirectly, we approached the herd until we were about fifty yards away. Taking advantage of the sun's angle and of the background, we saw through two telephoto lenses a classic scene of a most impressive species. One of the cows, followed by her calf, began to drift away from the group, but the bull was instantly alert to her impending escape and, with lowered antlers, hazed her back into the group. A second cow strayed and was likewise rounded up. Then a few others, feeling the first warmth of the September sun, began to bed down. We relaxed a little and that's when, suddenly, our bull galloped away to meet a second male that had just appeared.

The harem bull lunged head-on at the new arrival just as it emerged, dripping, from the Gibbon River. Although we could not clearly see the clash, we could hear the rattle of antlers and hooves pounding the turf. Even before we could aim cameras in their direction and focus, the issue was settled. The interloping bull retreated and ran off. The victor returned to his harem, bugled once more, and seemed to count his cows before bedding down. Only then did I remember that a grizzly bear might be somewhere in the vicinity. It was a typical September morning among Yellowstone's elk.

Neither smaller mule deer nor the larger moose are as abundant as elk in Yellowstone. But you might meet either anywhere. Once on the same day we found moose grazing on aquatic vegetation midstream in the Yellowstone River, as well as two thousand feet higher, in the next life zone, on the slope of Mount Washburn. Another good place to spot moose in the summer is in the Hayden Valley, very early or late in the day. Toward the end of summer a few gather in the Pelican Meadows at the mouth of Pelican Creek and along the Lewis River in the southern part of the park. I watch especially for mule deer in the Roosevelt Lodge area, around the Grand Canyon rim trails and, in late fall and winter, between Mammoth and Gardiner.

The foothills zone of northern Yellowstone may be the best area anywhere to see another American original, the pronghorn, or pronghorn antelope. At different times of the year the animals spread out from this favored

Above: *A black bear cub watches from a tree as its mother and a sibling forage in the meadow below.* **Right:** *Ground squirrels are ubiquitous around some campgrounds. This one was spooked by a passing coyote.*

area, moving far eastward into the Lamar Valley or even northward onto private property beyond the park. But at least some are almost always on hand to greet new arrivals around the North Entrance.

On mountains where they are hunted bighorn sheep are the wariest of all big game animals. But after decades of total protection Yellowstone sheep have became accustomed to people and make little effort to avoid them. One of the park's most outstanding wildlife shows, matching the September elk rut in drama and violence, is the annual November sheep rut on Mount Everts. One snowy afternoon I sat against a rock for shelter from a biting wind, and watched a dozen or more rams engaged in lunging, crashing, head-to-head duels all around me. Any single impact would seem enough to smash a sheep skull or scramble the brains inside. But most of these were multiple explosions from which the rams seemed unaffected; all was meant to determine breeding rights with bands of ewes grazing nearby. These females exhibited complete disinterest in the violent confrontations taking place all around them. Unfortunately this area of the park is now closed to the public due to poaching of trophy rams and the introduction of disease.

The Yellowstone wilderness (both within and beyond park boundaries) has given at least one endangered species a chance to come back from the edge of extinction. By about 1920 trumpeter swans had all but disappeared from America, but today about three hundred individuals live in Yellowstone and the surrounding ecosystem. In fact, the entire Rocky Mountain population winters in the Greater Yellowstone area. They have fared well enough since the 1970s to allow a few to be trapped for restocking elsewhere. The best place to see them in summer is along the Madison River.

Yellowstone hosts an abundance of other unique species—some you may have to look closely for. Four species of amphibians, six reptiles including the prairie rattlesnake (found only in the extreme north end), and over one hundred species of butterflies are found in Yellowstone Park. Two rare plants, Tweedy's sand verbena (on the shore of Yellowstone Lake) and Ross bent grass (in the Upper Geyser Basin), probably exist only within Yellowstone's boundaries.

One splendid Yellowstone native that travelers no longer see is the gray wolf. The last wolves in the park were shot or trapped by 1942. The Endangered Species Act of 1973 requires the federal government to try to reestablish the wolf in the park, and many feasibility studies have been conducted, scientific opinions and reports filed, and public hearings held, all favoring reintroduction as soon as possible. But as I write this no move has yet been made to do so. A powerful coalition of western ranchers and politicians, plus inertia, have killed every effort to reintroduce gray wolves to Yellowstone.

It's possible, however, that wolves might reintroduce *themselves* to the park as they expand their range southward from Canada and Montana. Currently, in late 1992, there are on record several unconfirmed wolf sightings in and around Yellowstone. In September 1992 an animal believed to be a coyote was shot just south of Yellowstone. Upon studying the carcass, wildlife biologists believe it to be that of a gray wolf. If further genetic tests reveal that the animal was indeed a wolf, it will be the first confirmed physical evidence of wolves in Yellowstone Country in decades.

Wild wolves, if reestablished in Yellowstone, could play their important roll of controlling the chronic overpopulations of elk and bison in the park. But they should be restored in the park simply because they belong in Yellowstone. Their night howling should be as much a part of the park experience as watching Old Faithful erupt on a glorious summer's day.

Cottontails are most often seen in the northern part of Yellowstone. This one lived near the administrative buildings at Mammoth.

We interrupted this badger's digging in the extreme northern section of Yellowstone. Badgers are numerous around ground squirrel colonies in the Yellowstone Valley north of the park.

A rare and exhilarating sight in Yellowstone is the elusive grizzly bear. An estimated 180 to 200 grizzlies currently roam the Greater Yellowstone Ecosystem.

Above: *Bison, like these near Old Faithful, tend to stay close to the warm hydrothermal areas during bitterly cold periods.* **Right:** *Yellow-bellied marmots are easily seen all summer long at the rock piles below Sheepeater Cliffs.*

Although mountain lions, or cougars, are rarely seen, a population of the secretive cats thrives (and may be increasing) in Yellowstone.

A bighorn ram rests on the lower slope of Gardner Canyon and is easily visible from the Gardiner-Mammoth road.

THE GREATER YELLOWSTONE ECOSYSTEM

In 1917 Emerson Hough, then one of America's foremost conservation writers, suggested in *The Saturday Evening Post* that vast areas surrounding Yellowstone National Park, being interrelated, should be annexed to the park. That may have been the first mention ever of a Greater Yellowstone Ecosystem (GYE) concept. But the United States was in the middle of the first World War, and there were other, more pressing problems on people's minds than the environment. Even today, in fact, there usually are.

In 1891, nineteen years after the park was established, Congress did set aside about 1.25 million acres as the Yellowstone Timberland Reserve, much of which is now national forest land. But it wasn't until very recent times that the idea of a Greater Yellowstone area gained wide acceptance. Today it is a reality, consisting of roughly thirty-two thousand square miles of the northern Rocky Mountains in Wyoming, Montana, and Idaho, a total area larger than that of South Carolina. Besides Yellowstone Park, the Greater Yellowstone Ecosystem includes Grand Teton National Park, three national wildlife refuges, and large portions of seven surrounding national forests. It is a conservation reserve of global importance. The vast area of the ecosystem outside Yellowstone Park rivals the great natural wonder and beauty that exists within its borders.

The national forest lands near Yellowstone include the highest peaks in both Wyoming (13,785-foot Gannett Peak) and Montana (12,799-foot Granite Peak), as well as one of the world's largest volcanic craters, Island Park Caldera in Idaho. The Greater Yellowstone area also offers critical habitat for grizzly bears and gray wolves (if wolves are reintroduced) and a better chance for both species to survive than does Yellowstone Park alone. No other region of the United States contains a greater population of big game animals: an estimated (in 1991) 87,000 mule deer; 70,000 elk; 7,000 bighorn sheep; 6,000 moose; 1,500 mountain goats; 3,000 black bears; 4,500 antelope; a few hundred grizzly bears; and many white-tailed deer. More endangered peregrine falcons, trumpeter swans, and bald eagles exist here than anywhere south of Alaska. Botanically speaking, much of the ecosystem remains to be examined and "discovered." Botanists did not find one of the most important bogs in the region until 1984. Five new species of plants have been discovered in the ecosystem since 1982 and others are in the process of being classified.

The abundance of natural resources in the GYE also has a down side. Much of it is heavily forested and under pressure from timber companies and politicians; far too much of it is being harvested to guarantee a sustained yield of timber. Overgrazing by cattle on some national forest lands is disgraceful, all of it at public expense. Perhaps even more potentially menacing is the threat to the treasure of minerals that exists in high places. There is constant pressure to extract the minerals, no matter what the consequences to the environment. If there is a bright spot here it is that recreation and tourism may be gradu-

From its source in Yellowstone, the Snake River flows southward through Grand Teton National Park. The fires of 1988 create a smoky sunset.

ally replacing logging, livestock, and mining in importance to local economies. Today's travelers to Yellowstone Park find that the wild beauty does not end at park gates.

From Yellowstone Lake on clear days three snow-capped peaks are easily visible far to the south. These are the Tetons, rising suddenly from the floor of Jackson Hole to 13,770 feet above sea level—the heart of Grand Teton National Park. For almost twenty years Peggy and I lived on the edge of the 310,000-acre park; it was an idyllic time for exploring a splendid high trail system, climbing through picturesque canyons to wilderness backcountry, morainal lakes, and meadows knee-deep in wildflowers. It is inconceivable to me that Grand Teton was not made a national park until seventy-eight years after the establishment of Yellowstone National Park.

Once on the subject, it is difficult not to write about Grand Teton Park, which is separated from Yellowstone Park by only a strip of the Bridger-Teton National Forest. I think of the autumn daybreaks and the rutting bull moose at Oxbow and Sawmill ponds; of hiking over Paintbrush Divide, along the Teton Crest Trail to Lake Solitude; of camping in Alaska Basin; of photographing the birth of a moose calf in my backyard and the pine martens that lived near the log cabin of Margaret Murie. She, her husband, Olaus, and brother-in-law Adolf were pioneers in the drive to establish wilderness areas in America.

One summer I hiked along the South Boundary Trail, paralleling the Snake River in southern Yellowstone Park, past hot springs seldom seen, to Heart Lake, and finally to Big Game Ridge. The highest parts of the ridge are prime summer range for elk, the same animals in fact that spend winters almost seventy miles away on the National Elk Refuge in Jackson Hole.

Long before Jackson Hole (hole was an old mountain man's word for "valley") was first invaded by the beaver trappers, vast herds of elk from their southern-most summer ranges in the GYE would migrate even farther south each fall through the length of the Snake River valley, where they found enough food to survive the sometimes brutal winters. These herds then returned to the GYE high country every spring. But their migration routes were blocked when the town of Jackson was settled. One year of exceedingly deep snow early in this century, an estimated ten thousand elk died of starvation. Many more were killed by ranchers protecting their haystacks. Still more were shot only to retrieve their teeth,

then popular in the eastern United States as good luck charms and key chain ornaments. Outcry by environmentally concerned citizens over the slaughter led in 1912 to the establishment of the thirty-seven-square-mile National Elk Refuge in Jackson Hole, where between 7,500 and 10,000 elk now spend the winter. The animals are fed alfalfa pellets to keep them from wandering farther south onto ranchlands. The feeding program is financed in part by the annual collection of antlers (shed by the bulls) by the local Boy Scouts. Koreans buy the antlers at an annual Jackson auction and grind them up, presumably to be used as aphrodisiacs.

Between Christmas and April 1 the elk massed on the refuge are both a profitable tourist attraction and a remarkable spectacle. Visitors can ride out right among the elk on horse-drawn sleighs with the Tetons as a backdrop. It is a scenic biomass without equal. It is also a very cold experience, because the temperature does not rise above zero on many windy winter days in Jackson Hole.

Two other national wildlife refuges are part of the Greater Yellowstone Ecosystem. Grays Lake, in Idaho, is barely within the southwestern boundary of the area. Surrounded by national forest land and the Caribou Mountains, Grays Lake is an important wetland sanctuary for many wild species. Most notably, it is a nesting area for between two hundred and three hundred pairs of sandhill cranes. It is also the "laboratory" where our friend, biologist Rod Drewien, conceived the idea of raising endangered whooping cranes by placing the eggs of captive whoopers in wild sandhill crane nests. So far, so good: More than a dozen whooping cranes have been raised to adulthood and have made annual winter migrations to New Mexico and beyond. But they have not yet mated.

Grays Refuge, not far from Soda Springs, is an excellent destination for birders. But to guarantee security for the nesting cranes, western grebes, and white-faced ibises, public access is limited to about five miles of refuge roads and connecting country roads, not always in the best of condition. Still, the place would have to be included on any list of best-but-least-known wildlife treasures.

Also in that category, although even more remote from busy tourist trails, is the Red Rock Lakes National Wildlife Refuge. It exists almost undiscovered in the wild and remote Centennial Valley of extreme southwestern Montana. It was here that a few pairs of trum-

Mule deer range over most of Yellowstone Country. This fawn, only a few weeks old, was photographed in June.

The colors of autumn are always stunning along the upper Snake River as September blends into October.

A rainbow follows a summer afternoon rain squall over the Absaroka Mountains and Paradise Valley, just north of Yellowstone.

The Grand Tetons are a dramatic backdrop for arrowleaf balsaroot.

An angler casts for cutthroat trout in a channel of the Snake River in Grand Teton Park, north of Moose.

peter swans were found after many believed that they had vanished from the Rocky Mountains—in fact, from all of North America. Now a fairly stable population of 200 to 250 of the thirty-pound waterfowl has been established. Even so, a traveler is not always assured of seeing them, because the species nests in the most remote places. But many other birds of the western mountains, prairies, and marshlands, plus moose and antelope, can be counted here.

About one-third of the refuge's sixty-seven square miles consists of a shallow lake, marshlands, and soggy meadows, with Red Rock Creek running through the middle. Summer is sometimes plagued by mosquitoes, and winter is a forbidding, though silent and exquisite, season. Snowfall averages about thirteen feet annually. In all the Greater Yellowstone Ecosystem few areas have an absolute wilderness aura to match this one.

Peggy and I are lucky that we do not have to drive far, and on unimproved roads, to stand in wilderness. A thirty-minute walk (or cross-country ski tour) from our back porch, past the band of whitetail deer that watches us suspiciously as soon as we open the door, takes us into the 930,000-acre Absaroka-Beartooth Wilderness

Area. If we kept hiking all summer or for several summers, we would pass through portions of the Gallatin, Custer, and Shoshone national forests, skirt hundreds of high-country lakes containing trout, and never once have to retrace our footsteps. It is simply a backpacker's and pack-tripper's paradise.

Outfitter Gene Wade, then of Cooke City, Montana, introduced me to this lonely, lofty backcountry before it was officially designated the Absaroka-Beartooth Wilderness Area under the United States Wilderness Act. Gene and I wandered to isolated places such as Hidden Lake, Grasshopper Glacier, Jorden and Fossil lakes, and anywhere else we might find rainbow, cutthroat, or golden trout. We caught—and over a campfire fried—our share, but what I remember most is the magnificent alpine scenery, wildflowers, thunderstorms, sunsets, and the bighorn sheep. Sometimes late in the day there was also a little saddle soreness, but coffee cooking over the next morning's campfire seemed to cure it.

I have left description of the national forests in this chapter for last because (except for the wilderness areas within) they are the least well-managed public lands within the Greater Yellowstone Ecosystem. Most of the local managers and forest rangers are wise and competent men and women, but the policies that come down from Washington, D.C., are often deplorable, allowing over-grazing of the land and over-harvesting of the timber.

One morning Peggy and I began a long-anticipated backpack trip from a trailhead just west of Teton Pass in the Bridger-Teton National Forest. Our plan was to hike northward into Grand Teton Park and follow the Teton Crest Trail along the main Teton Range. About three hours into the trip we came upon large areas where the ground had been trampled and the vegetation consumed as in the wake of a great cattle drive. I have seen wartime battle zones less badly torn up. Eventually even the trail was obliterated, and we had a difficult time finding our way around a very deep chasm, with no markers to guide us. Then we came upon the problem: a herd of five hundred to six hundred sheep. I do not know if they were in that area legally or illegally (we saw no sheepherders), but no matter; the damage was the same either way.

The fact is that sheep should never have been in that area at all, even if the owners paid the legal grazing fee, set by the U.S. Congress and low enough to be a sad joke. We have also found badly over-grazed areas in the Shoshone National Forest where the Forest Service today admits to granting grazing permits for twenty-seven thousand sheep, cattle, and horses. That is a number the land simply cannot sustain and still protect the watershed. Time and again we even have found signs of cattle grazing in the Absaroka-Beartooth Wilderness, where by law no domestic stock should ever be.

Nor is the Targhee National Forest of Idaho the best example of land management. North of Idaho Falls toward Island Park is a loop that passes one of the most lovely rainbow waterfalls in America, Mesa Falls of the Snake River. It is a favorite of calendar photographers, and no wonder. But drive a little farther back to the main highway and all you can see for miles and miles is clear-cut forests with piles of slash waiting to be burned on a damp day.

It is always a relief to hurry past this area to Harriman State Park, where the trumpeter swans share Henrys Fork of the Snake River, a world class trout stream, with summer's influx of trout anglers. But I never really feel that I am back in pure, undisturbed, wild America until I escape West Yellowstone's clutter and enter the west gate into Yellowstone Park.

Overleaf: One of the most photographed scenes in the Yellowstone ecosystem—or anywhere—is Oxbow Pond of the Snake River in Grand Teton Park, in fall foliage.

EXPERIENCING YELLOWSTONE

Many travelers pass right through Yellowstone every summer virtually without pause, seeing the park as just another place to check off on a long list. Blame some of that on our hurried lifestyle and some on the congestion and traffic jams that tourists find in the park during holiday seasons. One way to avoid the crowds is to schedule a trip for before or after the surge of human summer migration, from mid-May until mid-June, or after Labor Day. But even during peak travel times there are a few narrow, one-way roads onto which a visitor might briefly escape, including the Blacktail Butte road, the Firehole Flat drive, and the Firehole Lake drive. A scenic byway parallels Virginia Cascades and another almost encircles Bunsen Peak.

But there is another Yellowstone altogether, away from all the roads and concessions. Not far from the main arteries in almost any direction lies a wholly fresh world of wildflower meadows, colorful paint pots, petrified forests, and sweet solitude. I feel sorry for the tourists who do not lock up their cars, don hiking shoes, and explore on foot these places that many think of as the *real* Yellowstone.

Birding is a great excuse to travel the backcountry trails. Of the 160 or so species of birds found nesting in the park, about one-quarter are year-round residents. So it is possible to accumulate a fairly good list of northern Rocky Mountain species right here. The largest number of species can be counted from early June to mid-July and again during the second half of August. But

they are easier to spot and identify early than late because of brighter breeding plumage and greater activity then. Bird song is best enjoyed from late May through June when avian courtship is in full swing. June and July is the main nesting period. With the young of the year added to the summer population, the number of birds is highest in August, gradually dwindling through September and October until all of the migrant species are gone.

As an added bonus, the best bird guide ever compiled for an area of similar size is available for Yellowstone. Ornithologist Terry McEneaney's *Birds of Yellowstone* can make searching for birds a pleasure, or even a passion.

Yellowstone contains the kind of terrain that can make hiking the highest adventure throughout the summer. Advancing age has changed me from the long-distance trekker of years past into the day-tripper, but the rich rewards are undiminished. I recall the times I hiked deep into the Hellroaring Slopes country, up the Bechler River, or to Broad and Deep creeks with light fishing tackle along with the tent in my backpack, to enjoy the excellent trout fishing in all the waters. Now I am much more likely to retrace my footsteps over an old favorite trail such as a six-mile, three- or four-hour loop to Fairy Falls. To begin, we drive at daybreak to the trailhead on Fountain Flat Drive. From there we follow Fairy Creek upstream, through an area burned in the 1988 Yellowstone fires, to Imperial Geyser. From there it is another half mile to the base of two-hundred-foot

A chipmunk gathers ripe wild rose hips. The plant's red fruit is a favorite food of many other Yellowstone mammals and birds.

Riders in a pack train explore the alpine country of the Beartooth Mountains near the northeast corner of Yellowstone Park.

Fairy Falls, one of the highest water drops in the park. We almost always find elk along the return trail to Midway Geyser Basin, and once we came upon an elk cow with a calf born only minutes earlier. We watched from a distance while the wet, spotted, unsteady baby finally managed to stand up on wobbly legs. While it nursed for the first time, the mother gently licked its behind as is instinctive.

Late one afternoon a year following the 1988 fires, the summer thunderheads that had been building up unnoticed by us turned into a sudden violent thunderstorm. We hurried and then practically ran back toward the trailhead and our parked car through a strip of the burned area. A wild wind whined through the skeletons of lodgepole pines, toppling one of the potential widowmakers directly in our path. It was a sobering moment in an otherwise exciting, if damp, experience.

Situated between 44 and 45 degrees north latitude, Yellowstone is exactly halfway between the Equator and the North Pole, which would seem to place it in the world's temperate zone. But since there is a net loss of about three and a half degrees Fahrenheit for every one thousand feet of elevation above sea level, and since

Yellowstone is mostly a high plateau, it is a cool to cold region. Its climate can be described as harsh, with great temperature variations between day and night and between summer and winter. In addition, the southern portion of the park receives high annual precipitation, mostly in the form of winter snowfall, while the northern part is much drier. The foothills area around Gardiner may even be snow-free for long periods in winter.

The point is that the longer and higher the hike, the more important it is, even in mid-summer, to be prepared for changeable weather. You may want to carry a sweater and foul weather gear in a daypack. And nothing can contribute more to an enjoyable trip than hiking shoes that fit perfectly and are comfortable and well-broken in before you hit the trails.

An entire book could be written about Yellowstone's trail system. Even the hardiest hiker would have trouble completing all the trails, even in a lifetime devoted to it. But two steep, switchbacking three-mile trails deserve special mention because of their easy accessibility and the unique chance offered to reach the alpine life zone of the park. From trailheads on the Chittenden Road and at Dunraven Pass the two paths lead upward through

Above left: *In late springtime on Mount Washburn, a male blue grouse in breeding plumage courts a female in dense brush.* **Above right:** *Wildflowers along Tower Creek add a dash of color to a misty autumn day.* **Right:** *In June, mountainsides are carpeted with yellow arrowleaf balsaroot.*

Every evening in summer, guests of Roosevelt Lodge arrive at evening cookouts via vintage Yellowstone stagecoaches.

a spectacular display of mountain wildflowers that reach their peak in July. They converge at a fire lookout atop 10,243-foot Mount Washburn. From here the view of Yellowstone Country is magnificent. The bighorn sheep you usually meet along the way, especially near the summit, will not mind the wind and cold as much as you do, so carry a sweater or windbreaker. We also always carry water to drink, which is sound advice for any long walk in the park. *Yellowstone Trails*, a booklet by Mike Marshall, can be purchased in visitor centers and is a valuable guide.

There is no shortage of organized outdoor activities in Yellowstone, some of the best of which are free. Especially for first-time visitors I recommend joining one of the daily ranger-led interpretive hikes to points of interest or beauty. Most of these are slow-paced and not rigorous. Each is a short course in some phase of natural history, from geothermal activity and the effects of forest fires to bird and mammal behavior. Up-to-date copies of the newsletter *Discover Yellowstone* are available at ranger stations and visitors centers, and they list the locations and times of each of these hikes.

Fishing in Yellowstone Park is also without charge, although it is necessary to obtain a free permit. (To fish

outside the park you will need a valid state fishing license.) Many outdoor scribes, myself included, have in the past described Yellowstone Park fishing as the best in the United States. That is no longer true, although serious competent anglers can do very well in several rivers such as the Madison and parts of the Yellowstone and Firehole, which are classic trout waters. The truth is that better sport for large trout exists elsewhere in the Greater Yellowstone Ecosystem, such as the Madison River below Quake Lake to Three Forks, Montana; Henrys Fork of the Snake River in Island Park, Idaho; and the Yellowstone River from Yankee Jim Canyon to Livingston, Montana. Most park river fishing is with artificial flies only. It is illegal to use live or dead natural baits.

Trolling for cutthroat trout with artificial lures in Yellowstone Lake is fairly good throughout the summer. Boats and fishing guides can be chartered at the Bridge Bay Marina, and visitors can launch their own boats or canoes at Bridge Bay. Keep in mind, though, that the weather here is unpredictable: Sudden squalls and high winds can develop without much warning. The largest lake in the United States, at an elevation of

Steller's jays splash bright blue color across the Yellowstone scene. They're especially visible around campgrounds.

nearly eight thousand feet, should never be taken lightly.

A serious trout angler sampling the Yellowstone region would do well to first check into one of the excellent tackle shops, where fluent fly fishing is spoken, for the latest best information and to learn which fly patterns are currently hot. These shops, which also arrange guide service, are located in Ashton, Idaho, and West Yellowstone, Gardiner, and Livingston, Montana. Dan Bailey's tackle shop in Livingston is almost an ardent angler's national monument.

Canoeing and float tripping are not permitted on park rivers, but these craft can be launched just outside the park. The Yellowstone River from Gardiner north through Yankee Jim Canyon is turbulent for whitewater rafting, and one outfitter conducts trips through most of the summer.

Although Yellowstone is not a good boating destination, it is worth carrying a canoe on cartop carriers for one reason only: to launch at Lewis Lake, cross to the far side, and then paddle up the Lewis River to where it drains Shoshone Lake. I have made the trip, with time to spare for fishing, in one day. But it is far better to obtain a free backcountry camping permit (necessary for any backcountry camping anywhere in the park) and make a longer adventure of it. One of my most intimate glimpses of Yellowstone grizzly bears, a female nursing twin cubs on a grassy bank in warm sunshine, occurred as I drifted silently downstream. My partner and I rounded a bend suddenly and were barely thirty feet from the three. So unexpected was the sight that I forgot to use the camera hanging around my neck. We were just past them, gripping the paddles with white knuckles, when the mother bear realized she was not alone. A paddle stroke or two and we were out of sight—and probably out of mind, too.

The Lewis–to–Shoshone Lake return trip is certainly among the purest wilderness canoeing adventures of the Rockies. And one of the best park bargains is an annual five-day, all-expense canoe trip on Lewis and Shoshone lakes offered by the non-profit Yellowstone Institute for about three hundred dollars. The institute sponsors about fifty two- to five-day seminars and field programs on many natural history subjects led by experts in each field, including general ecology, wildflowers, geothermal phenomena, tracking mammals, flora and fauna, and wildlife photography. Each of these costs one hundred dollars or less. There are special two-day family programs

and participants can rent cabins on site for very low rates.

It is no secret that during the busy summer months Yellowstone's campgrounds are constantly full. "No vacancy" signs are posted everywhere by noon and sometimes even before. Of course that is an inconvenience, but not a catastrophe. The numerous U.S. Forest Service and commercial campgrounds that exist within easy driving distance of all park gateways are rarely full to capacity. In addition, many of these U.S.F.S. sites offer more space and privacy than those in the park. Also, the commercial campgrounds have electric plug-ins, showers, and other amenities. Only one campground within Yellowstone, at Fishing Bridge, has electrical facilities for hard-sided camping units.

The main concessionaire in Yellowstone Park, operator of all lodgings, is TW Recreational Services. Besides the accommodations at Old Faithful, Mammoth, Tower-Roosevelt, Canyon, Lake, and Grant Villages, TW offers daily guided trail rides on horseback from the first three places mentioned. Every summer evening near Roosevelt there are western-style barbecues prepared some distance from the lodge area that the diner can reach either on horseback or via a vintage stagecoach. A few lucky ones may ride beside the driver on a high slab bench. It's a great opportunity to experience the Yellowstone of an earlier time.

It is perfectly possible and often a good idea to explore Yellowstone without ever sleeping one night in the park. The many resorts and guest ranches surrounding Yellowstone in Montana and Wyoming make it possible. Many organize pack trips into the backcountry during which participants never see another traveler. They revel in the salmon-colored sunsets around a fragrant campfire, sleep soundly under canvas, and sip hot, boiled coffee while the morning mists rise from the meadows all around them. They visit lonely hot springs and the summer range of elk and grizzlies that auto travelers never suspect exist. A summertime pack trip deep into the Yellowstone wilderness can be the most unforgettable experience of a person's lifetime.

I must say something else here about the wildlife any Yellowstone explorer is certain to meet. Each summer from fifteen to twenty visitors are injured by everything from ground squirrels (biting the fingers of children who feed them) to elk (which have stomped a few photograpers who press too near during the rut). Buffaloes gore or trample an average of five tourists a year, and

Silky phacelia is one of many species of wildflowers that grow along the highway to Dunraven Pass, peaking in July.

not because they are mean-spirited beasts. The victims, some gravely injured, violated the animals' limit of tolerance, and the creatures brushed them aside. So be advised.

The best way to explore Yellowstone is on foot—your horse's or your own—and never to leave anything behind except footprints.

Overleaf: In a golden meadow near the West Thum Geyser Basin, a bull elk bugles a calliope challenge during the fall rut.

A solitary skier glides over Upper Geyser Basin, returning to Snow Lodge in late afternoon.

PHOTOGRAPHING YELLOWSTONE

Very few travelers enter Yellowstone Park without carrying a camera in their car or duffel. In fact, more and more of them bring along very sophisticated photo equipment, the latest in point-and-shoot cameras with autofocus lenses. The amount of money spent on film must be astronomical, and yet well worth it. Photographing Yellowstone is pure pleasure. It's a tradition that began with William Henry Jackson during a U.S. Geological Survey expedition led by F.V. Hayden in 1871.

Carrying his bulky box camera and wooden tripod on pack mules, and using fragile, glass film plates, Jackson labored all summer long to make a photo record of a region very few had even heard about. He developed his film in a tent, often on a windy mountain ridge. Keeping his equipment dry was a constant major problem. But Jackson's black and white pictures were remarkable even by today's standards. All the climbing and hard work must have been good for him—he lived to be almost one hundred years old. Without specifically meaning to do so, that pioneer photographer infected many Americans with the national park idea.

Perhaps inevitably, growth of the American park system paralleled the gradual improvement in photographic gear and techniques. Most of the early Yellowstone tourists came armed with box cameras one-eighth the size of Jackson's. As more and more Yellowstone visitors returned home with better, more vivid photos, Americans became familiar with the park and its natural beauty.

In 1914 an avid amateur cameraman, Stephen Tyng Mather, was made director of national parks. It may have been the best appointment ever to the system. Mather sensed that good photography could be used to expand the park concept well beyond Yellowstone to other areas of the West that desperately needed protection.

One of Mather's first acts was to hire photo pro H. T. Cowling and send him on a year-long tour of western park areas. Although travel was still slow and laborious, Cowling had it easier than Jackson. Roads were being built to accommodate Henry Ford's new mass-produced automobiles, and photo gear was lighter and less bulky. Although Cowling's name is not well remembered now, thousands of our parents and grandparents first learned of Yellowstone and other parks from his sharp and inspired images.

Steve Mather later hired another photographer to publicize the national parks. Originally, Herbert Gleason was a frail and sickly preacher who resigned his calling, he said, only when "divine guidance" thrust a camera in his hands. The vocational change proved miraculous. In no time at all he was scaling national park peaks with fifty pounds of film and lenses on his back. Working until 1937, he accumulated a file of about six thousand negatives, which was extremely good production for that period. (By contrast, using modern, high-tech equipment, Peggy and I shoot two or three times that many exposures, of 35mm color film, every year.)

No traveler who ever met Gleason on a Yellowstone trail or elsewhere ever forgot him. A purist, he would

A bull elk along the Lamar River stares back at a photographer traveling on snowshoes.

Above: *A Yellowstone red squirrel gathers cones from an evergreen before the onset of winter.* **Right:** *Squirreltail barley is one of the hardy grassland plants that grows in Paradise Valley and in the northernmost parts of the park.*

never include people in pristine wilderness scenes. But later, when Gleason was shooting for *National Geographic* editor Gilbert Grosvenor, that purism caused conflict. Grosvenor wanted a human figure in every picture to give it depth, and, as always, the editor's position prevailed. But in Gleason's *National Geographic* photos, that human figure almost always turned out to be Gleason himself; his rangy silhouette and long, muttonchop sideburns became almost as familiar to *Geographic* readers as the magazine's yellow-bordered covers.

So today's many enthusiastic Yellowstone photographers evolved from just a few determined pioneers who had one characteristic in common: They knew a spectacular landscape and park when they saw it.

Photographing in Yellowstone is one activity anyone can pursue easily and well, especially given the quality of modern cameras and film. Now it is possible to shoot consistently good or even outstanding pictures, with simple and inexpensive gear.

Any camera for outdoor or adventure filming should be convenient to carry and neither too heavy nor too bulky. It should be sturdy, reliable, fast to use, and able to withstand a fair amount of rough handling and abuse. It should function in cold as well as in hot and damp weather. It should "feel" good, fitting comfortably in your hands. All these specifications translate into just one type of camera: the versatile single lens reflex (hereafter SLR) camera. All the photos in this book were made with 35 SLRs (35 refers to the most common and readily available film size, 35mm).

Keep in mind that not all serious nature photographers, pros or amateurs, prefer 35 SLRs. Specialists in grand landscapes and still lifes often opt for medium- or large-format equipment. Those heavier cameras use film larger than 35mm, from 120 film size (medium format) to the large studio type cameras that use sheet rather than roll film. Of course the larger and heavier the gear, the less it normally suits an active photographer who wanders far over Yellowstone trails. Larger formats are also a distinct disadvantage for shooting wildlife and motion.

The great advantage of the SLR camera is that the subject is viewed and focused directly through the single lens. You capture on film exactly what you see in the viewfinder the instant you expose the film. Most SLRs also have a focal plane shutter (a shutter that lies just in front of the film at the back of the camera) that allows a top shutter speed of 1/1,000 second. Some now have shutter speeds to 1/2,000 or even 1/4,000 second, but these are faster than most photographers ever need. A bewildering number of 35 SLRs are on the market nowadays—most are marvels of technology beyond comprehension, and selecting the best one is nearly impossible. Nevertheless, I would not advise buying a 35 SLR unless it belongs to a complete photo system that includes a range of interchangeable lenses from wide angle to telephoto, a camera motor drive (to advance film), speed lights, and other accessories.

One thing that is essential when shooting nature is never having to look away from your camera's viewfinder to make exposure settings or other adjustments. All exposure information should be exhibited right there in the viewfinder. The more you must attend to extraneous details, the more you are distracted and lose valuable concentration. So an accurate, built-in exposure meter (with the option not to use it at certain times) is vital to me. I also think that it is necessary to have automatic focusing available in a camera system, although I don't use it all the time. But when shooting wildlife or other action, autofocusing cameras and/or lenses can freeze moving subjects in far sharper focus, faster than is possible manually. The ideal 35 SLR should also be equipped with a motor drive to advance film (and rewind it) automatically.

Perhaps more important than which camera you choose is the manufacturer's manual that comes with every new one. Studying the manual carefully, and thereby really understanding how your camera works, can make all the difference between a stunning photo of Old Faithful that really thrills you and one you toss in the waste basket.

A camera is no better than the lens affixed to it. Lenses make or break pictures. To be able to shoot everything in the Yellowstone ecosystem, from wildflowers or insect closeups to the large mammals and landscapes, you'll need more than one lens. Peggy and I always carry a variety of lenses of different focal-lengths (focal length is the distance from the front of the lens to the film inside the camera).

The lens sold with most new 35 SLRs is the 50mm, presumably because its perspective is most nearly like that of the human eye. We use this one least often. On long hikes, when every ounce in a backpack counts, we don't even carry the 50mm. It's a good idea when buying a new 35 SLR to buy the camera body alone, without a lens. Then purchase separately those specific lenses you need.

Today's fine zoom lenses with variable focal lengths can replace several fixed focus lenses and reduce the gear you carry. If limited to just one lens, we would choose a zoom of 80mm to 200mm. This size lens serves well for most scenic photography and for some wildlife photos as well.

We have used telephoto lenses for as much as 90 percent of our Yellowstone photography; medium telephotos (70mm to 100mm) for scenes and landscapes and longer telephotos (300mm to 600mm) for wildlife.

Telephoto lenses have longer than normal focal length (longer than 50mm), magnifying the subject on the film and seeming to bring it closer. For example, the image of a deer in your viewfinder will be twice as large with a 100mm telephoto as with a 50mm lens. With a 200mm telephoto the deer will be four times as large as with the 50mm, or twice as large as with a 100mm, and so on. Because you do not have to approach as near a wild creature as you do with a shorter lens, a long lens is the invaluable device that makes wildlife photography possible. Telephotos enable anyone to shoot shy, wild creatures without frightening them, and without violating Yellowstone Park restrictions on approaching too near to any wildlife.

For photographing most Yellowstone creatures we depend on two telephoto lenses: a 300mm and a 400mm, either of which usually fills the viewfinder with one of the larger mammals. At times we also use a 600mm telephoto that enlarges the subject twelve times, but it is too large and heavy to carry very far. Remember that the longer the telephoto, the slower it tends to be and the more the slightest camera movement is exaggerated, resulting in a blurred and indistinct picture. To avoid this we always use a sturdy collapsible tripod with telephoto lenses of 300mm or longer. In Yellowstone it is often possible to shoot from an open car window, using a pillow, bean bag, or rolled up sweater as a cushion between the bottom of the lens and the window sill.

To increase the focal length of our telephoto lenses, we also carry 1.4X and 2X lens extenders, also called teleconverters. When mounted between camera and lens a 1.4X extender converts a 200mm lens to a 280mm lens; a 2X extender converts a 200mm to a 400mm lens. Extenders are small enough to fit into a shirt pocket, but

there is a penalty for using them. The 2X entails the loss of two f-stops in exposure. In other words, more light will be needed when using a 2X extender; thus, it might not work well in low-light conditions.

To shoot very small subjects we carry a macro lens. Designed especially for closeup photography, but useful as a normal lens, a macro or micro lens allows very close lens-to-subject focusing without accessory equipment. It is very difficult to shoot wildflowers, insects, or mushrooms, for example, without a 55mm or 100mm macro lens, either of which can also be used to shoot scenics.

Wide-angle lenses are used to shoot certain scenes or steep landscapes that are very near the photographer, or to shoot great panoramas. Often the short focal length has allowed us to shoot subjects we could not back away from. The depth of field of wide-angle lenses is greater: You can achieve in sharp focus everything from the immediate foreground to infinity. But wide-angles can also be deceptive. Unless you're very careful, you can distort a subject or be tempted to include too much area in one picture and thus lose impact.

There are two types of color film available: positive film for slides and negative film for prints. Manufacturers generally use the suffix "-chrome" to label slide film (Kodachrome[tm], Ektachrome[tm], Fujichrome[tm]) and the suffix "-color" to indicate print film (Kodacolor[tm], Ektacolor[tm], Fujicolor[tm]). We strongly recommend slide film because the color is almost always richer and more true. Excellent prints can be made from slides.

Both slide and print films come in a variety of speeds, from ASA/ISO 25, the slowest, to ASA/ISO 1000, the fastest readily available. Every film container indicates the film's speed rating, or sensitivity to light. Slow film reacts slowly to light and is best on bright Yellowstone days. Fast film reacts more quickly to light and is usually the choice on dreary days or in deep shade. As a rule of thumb, consider ASA/ISO 100 as a medium-speed, all-purpose choice. However, one quick survey of professional photographers shooting in Yellowstone on sunny days revealed that a majority preferred Kodachrome 64, on the slow side, day in and day out.

Almost as important as your camera, film, and lens is how best to carry them on Yellowstone trails. There are three alternatives, the choice depending on how far afield you plan to travel. (A camera hanging loosely on a strap around the neck is not an option!) The simplest and in many ways the handiest is the belt or fanny pack, which

An adult river otter prepares to eat a freshly caught trout. Look for otters along portions of rivers that remain unfrozen throughout the winter.

For winter wildlife photography, Peggy Bauer uses her ski poles as a handy bipod.

Canada geese are a common sight in the park. Many pairs nest in Yellowstone, and many overwinter here, never crossing park borders.

Above: *Of all the waterfalls in the park, Tower Fall may be the loveliest, especially early on a bright summer morning.*
Right: *Golden-mantled ground squirrels scamper around overlooks and parking areas, where they are joined by ravens and Clark's nutcrackers.*

fits snugly around the waist and can accommodate a limited amount of film and accessories. Belt packs are fine on shorter hikes when the load is light.

A photo vest or jacket is as handy as a belt pack, but it accommodates much more gear in separate, easily accessible compartments and pockets. Some jackets even have drop seats for sitting on damp ground, ventilated backs, and strap attachments for small tripods.

For a whole day or longer in the backcountry, a backpack is the obvious choice. Our longtime favorite has been a lightweight, exterior-frame model with many pockets. It is roomy enough to tote all the camera gear we are likely to need for an extended period. With two backpacks, Peggy and I can carry freeze-dried food, extra socks, rain gear, a two-person tent, and a double sleeping bag. Foul weather is no stranger to Yellowstone, so we seal all photo equipment in individual ziplock plastic bags or in light plastic supermarket sacks.

More than a century ago Americans had only the fine images of pioneer photographer William Jackson to prove that Yellowstone existed out there on the western frontier. Nowadays we all can see the park for ourselves and make our own memories of paradise in exquisite color. And that is a whole lot better.

THE FIRES OF
YELLOWSTONE

Midway through breakfast on September 7, 1988, guests at Old Faithful Inn were urged to pack their belongings immediately and leave the area. During the two previous days temperature inversions had smothered the region with such a dense pall of smoke that no one knew exactly how near a forest blaze, called the North Fork Fire, had actually burned. Few of those remaining in the vicinity of Old Faithful that morning will ever forget the nightmare.

Ranger-naturalist Carl Schreier, on duty at the adjacent visitor center, later recalled his experience. "I have fought forest fires before, but none to remotely match this one roaring out of the south. Flames from a mile-wide firestorm crackled over three hundred feet high. I saw a bomber plane drop loads of retardant right on a blaze near the employees' housing area, but it had no effect. I thought everything in [the fire's] path would have to go."

When the wall of fire, whipped by high winds, reached the housing complex, it arced almost one thousand feet over an open, asphalt-paved area to ignite trees on the opposite side. Schreier ran to his house trailer to try to retrieve personal property, but had to retreat when flames licked through the window. At the same time the last "strike team," a fire truck and crew that had been dousing buildings with water, realized it was past time to clear out. So Schreier was left behind and thereby became the only on-site witness to what followed at Old Faithful.

Fortunately he was experienced, fairly well equipped, and, so to speak, cool. He was dressed completely in fireproof clothing, from his shoes and gloves to his hard hat. Schreier also had three protective metal foil tents, which fire fighters call shake-and-bake shelters, for emergency use if he was overtaken by flames. He hooked up several hoses left behind and attached them to fire hydrants. During the next hour and a half, with the earth burning all around, the young naturalist fought the fight of his life, spraying everything in range. His closest call came when flames crawled beneath a fuel oil storage tank, but Schreier hosed them away.

"The sky was as dark as night," Schreier told me. One tongue of flame leaped over him and the buildings he had just hosed. His eyes burned. He choked, held his breath, and tried to drink from the hose spray while red embers fell in a shower all around him. The carbon monoxide he inhaled would later confine him to a hospital.

Eventually a platoon of soldiers returned to join the battle of Old Faithful. Schreier sat exhausted in the desolate, blackened scene. He felt relief, but not exhilaration. Through the smoke he occasionally could see the empty Old Faithful Inn still standing, undamaged.

Peggy and I watched that same firestorm from a less frightening viewpoint. We were photographing elk at nearby Biscuit Basin when the billowing, cauliflower cloud of smoke on the horizon became a mustard-colored funnel rising miles into the sky. As we watched, the funnel raced closer and closer at an astonishing speed

In the summer of 1988, fire smoldered in a woods along Indian Creek. Later a strong wind reignited the fire.

A great horned owl perches before a charred stump along Lewis River. The woods here was burned during the 1988 fires.

Wildflowers were the first sign of regrowth, here on Mount Washburn and elsewhere, during spring 1989 following the 1988 Yellowstone fires.

until we could see the orange fire beneath. The sun was blotted out and the scene appeared like nightfall. Then the sun reappeared as a crimson ball as the smoke thinned before its face. It was a scene of terrible beauty, of apocalypse now. I recall thinking that Hiroshima must have looked something like this from afar. All at once we realized that this firestorm was headed toward Old Faithful and also toward us, alone at Biscuit Basin. Strangely, even as it became very dark, the elk did not interrupt their grazing. But we folded up tripods and drove quickly northward until we reached Madison Junction. We expected never again to walk through the historic lobby of Old Faithful Inn.

How the then-eighty-five-year-old tinderbox, a hallowed American landmark, withstood the wind, smoke, and passing firestorm remains a miracle of that Black Wednesday. Everything seemed to mitigate against its survival. It was made completely of wood, which had dried over the years. And the basic design was really a ready-made chimney, with a large central area open to the roof line, skirted by wooden balconies on all sides. Seventeen buildings located nearby had been leveled. Probably what protected the hotel was the vast paved

parking lot around it that acted as a fire break. In any case, saving the Inn was one victory in what seemed to be a summer-long war against fire in the world's premier national park. For the first time since President Grant opened it to all citizens in 1872, the park was completely closed to tourists.

For more than three months, beginning in June, nine separate fires burned within the Greater Yellowstone Ecosystem. Half started outside the park, one by sparks from a logger's chain saw, another by sparks from a powerline snapped by a falling tree. The exact causes of the rest are unknown. From time to time the gateway communities of West Yellowstone, Gardiner, Silver Gate, and Cooke City were threatened by blazes visible from their main streets. Before fall, from one-third to more than one-half of all park lands would be scorched or burned to the ground.

On that Black Wednesday alone ten thousand acres may have gone up in smoke as firestorms advanced with bewildering speed. By September up to ten thousand men and women, including two thousand army troops and U.S. Marines, plus an astronomical amount of equipment, including 229 pumper trucks and 27 helicopters,

Black bears just out of hibernation find the desiccated carcass of a bull elk—the victim of either a brutal winter or the Yellowstone fires.

were fighting a desperate battle to save the park. Accurate accounting may never be made, but the bill for fighting the Yellowstone fires exceeds 150 million dollars. The Yellowstone Ecosystem fires may have been the most extensive fires in the memory of humankind.

What could have caused the devastating blaze? The year 1988 was the hottest and driest in Yellowstone Park's 116-year history, drier even than the Dust Bowl years of the 1930s. Furthermore, following a low snowfall winter in 1987–1988, almost no measurable rain fell from May until September. Forest scientists routinely measure the moisture content in forest logs, and by mid-July the moisture in northwestern Wyoming was almost 50 percent below the twenty-five-year average. In other words, the state was set for easy ignition in the summer of 1988.

At the same time a Yellowstone management plan to permit natural (lightning-caused) fires to burn under natural conditions had been in place since 1972. Only fires that threatened human life and property or wildlife were to be controlled. The same policy was in place in other national parks of the West. The rationale for the "natural burn" policy was twofold: Fires have always been a reality in our forests and prairies, and they are

nature's way of renewing itself and rejuvenating vegetation. But it may have been a mistake to follow too long the park management plan when drought conditions were so bad.

To make matters worse, for sixty years before the 1972 management plan fires had been suppressed in Yellowstone, allowing an abnormal amount of fuel (deadfalls, decaying trees, and debris) to accumulate on the ground. This contributed to the intensity of the fires wherever they spread.

Peggy and I made several lengthy trips into the park during the fires. Each was physically exhausting, leaving us with red eyes and pine-smoked lungs. We photographed the fires from a vantage near enough to barely tolerate the intense heat. We followed fire-fighters to observe as they toiled at their dirty, dangerous job.

One afternoon, separated from a weary fire crew, we were almost encircled by a wind-driven inferno near Sheepeater Cliffs and knew a few minutes of terror before finding our way out. That same day we learned that a firestorm advancing on a broad front can create a monstrous noise like that of several jumbo jets taking off at once. The closer to the fires we stood, the harder it was

The destruction of the 1988 fires is evident in these before-and-after photos of a pond just south of Mammoth and east of the park highway.

to justify them.

We realized early that a forest fire is an unpredictable living thing. It may move slowly, creeping along and crackling as if no more than a nuisance, easy to stamp out. Then almost imperceptibly it can gain speed, quickly becoming a roaring, consuming, dreadful machine impossible to suppress. To call some fires awesome is to understate the case.

We were especially interested in how Yellowstone's wildlife coped with the spreading blazes. Several newspapers in the Rocky Mountain region reported a heavy toll of big game, of deer, elk, and bison being trapped by the flames. Rumors circulated that park officials were disposing of animal carcasses in mass graves so that the public would never find these victims of a "let-burn" policy that was becoming more and more bitterly criticized. As usual, politicians had the most to say, and most of it was misleading or simply wrong.

Besieged by citizen concern over the alleged animal casualties, Wyoming governor Mike Sullivan sent a team of biologists to fly over northwest Wyoming backcountry in late September 1988 for an accurate report. They counted thirteen dead elk that appeared to have been trapped between a deliberately set backburn (a fire set to stop the advance of another, larger blaze) and the rapidly advancing Mink Creek fire. A healthy grizzly was feeding on one of the carcasses. On October 6 park officials announced that about one hundred dead elk had been located in the southwestern section of Yellowstone. The animals were probably overwhelmed by smoke or killed by the rapidly approaching Wolf Lake fire a month earlier. Up-to-date reports from aircraft were often impossible to get due to the large amounts of drifting smoke that obscured many parts of the ground. An estimated thirty-two thousand elk were then summering in the park.

I talked to many fire-fighters who had worked throughout the summer in various parts of Yellowstone, and I did not find one who had personally witnessed any animal casualties. Nor did Peggy or I find any carcasses or any injured animals while we photographed in the park. Park rangers and biologists agree that even severe fires do not pose a threat to most large mammals because they are able to evade the flames. We photographed seemingly unconcerned trumpeter swans preening in the Madison River in a pall of smoke as fires burned in the immediate background. The images on film seem as strange today as they did at the time.

From past experience, though, biologists know that widespread, fast-moving blazes such as those in Yellowstone will take a considerable toll of some creatures not as well equipped to escape as elk. A list of some of those includes blue and ruffed grouse, chickadees, snowshoe hares, mice and voles, chipmunks, porcupines, weasels, and martens. As many may perish from asphyxiation as from burning in the flames. One day while photographing along the front edge of the flames, I watched pine voles scurrying aimlessly as if trying to escape the hot ground. Some darted back toward the fiery area.

The real crisis for the large animals came months after the fire, when winter gripped the land. A large portion of the Yellowstone landscape had already been over-browsed and over-grazed before the flames ignited. Also, populations of elk and bison were at a fifty-year peak, and would have presented a problem even during a wet year. So from January through March of 1989, with much of the animals' winter survival food in ashes, winter kill was estimated at between eight thousand and twelve thousand large mammals. In one way it was a tragic loss. But in the long term it would reduce big game numbers to the carrying capacity of the range.

The bears fared marginally better than the hooved animals. Some must have entered hibernation in November with insufficient fat stored to survive until spring. The survivors emerged lean and ravenous in April to find scorched land without the green grasses, sedges, and herbs they require. Instead they found protein readily available in the elk and bison carcasses. A few wandered outside the park in search of food and got into trouble with ranchers.

All of the most famous natural attractions of Yellowstone survived unaltered. Old Faithful Inn and the other historic lodgings opened on schedule in 1989. Some trails had to be closed, though only temporarily. But much of the wilderness scenery was drastically changed. Vast tracts of black tree trunks stood on mountain slopes that once were green. Forest regrowth did not begin as soon or as vigorously as park officials had predicted and hoped, although burned grasslands (as at Swan Flat and in the Lamar Valley) were as green as ever in the spring of 1989. In time undergrowth and exquisite wildflowers did appear on the floors of many dead forests, but the ground of the most thoroughly burned areas, those that had been sterilized, remained nearly

Above: *A bobcat appears briefly on a charred log to drink before suddenly evaporating back into the forest.* **Left:** *Driven by high afternoon winds, fire races through the crowns of lodgepole pine forest in the southern part of Yellowstone.*

bare three years later. In the future plant communities more varied than the unbroken stands of lodgepole pines should grow here.

Toward the end of September 1988, soft autumn rains and then an early snow began to fall, the first precipitation in many months across the Yellowstone wilderness. Gradually the fires were snuffed out. But in October we still found scarlet embers alive inside the trunk of a giant Douglas fir. Winter winds toppled that tree, and snow dampened and then killed the last of the fireglow. Some critics still contend that the natural burn policy was a failure. But lightning-caused fires burned only until late July, when political pressure caused the government to launch its all-out attack. Even then, fighting such fires as the Hellroaring and North Fork blazes by every possible means did not slow their progress any more quickly than unsuppressed natural fires. Most scientific reviews have supported the hands-off concept.

The bottom line is that the summer of 1988 did not destroy our oldest national park. But it may have sewn the seeds for a new green beginning.

Overleaf: A ground fire rages near Norris Geyser Basin, consuming all standing trees, as well as brush and deadfalls, in its path.

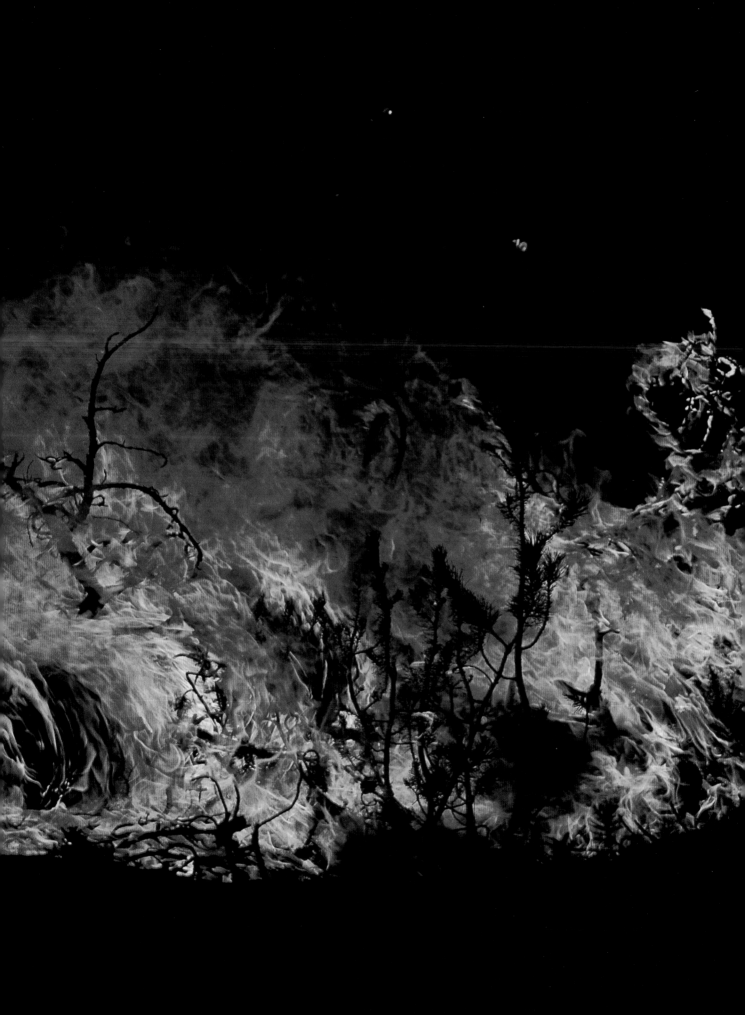

THE RIVERS OF YELLOWSTONE

Following the 1988 Yellowstone fires, among the greatest fears of scientists and fishermen and -women was the impact the fires might eventually have on the clear, sweet rivers running through the land. The Yellowstone is the longest free-flowing, undammed river left in America and an incomparable national treasure. Would silt washing down from the now barren hillsides affect the delicate ecology of the waters? What would this do to native species of fish? Landslides from badly burned hillsides did dam the Gibbon River until they were bulldozed away. And during 1989 some streams ran much more roily, much later in the season than usual. We still do not know the long-term answers to these questions.

Of all nature's forces, few affect the landscape more than running water. The Yellowstone River is the largest of the many fast-flowing mountain rivers that have carved Yellowstone Country into a wilderness of stream-cut valleys flowing outward in all directions. As is typical of the northern Rocky Mountains, a fairly high to very high rainfall is common over the Yellowstone plateau. Any precipitation that does not evaporate or is not absorbed for new plant growth runs off and, because the mountain ranges here are steep, it drains swiftly. Some of the Greater Yellowstone Ecosystem waters end up in the Pacific Ocean via the Snake and Columbia rivers. Some drain southward via the Green and Colorado rivers toward the Gulf of California. But most are destined for the Gulf of Mexico via the Yellowstone, Missouri, and Mississippi rivers, which carry them first east to Lake Sakakawea in North Dakota and then south to their destination.

Water from rain or snow dissolves minerals in the soil and alters others chemically. It also carries tiny particles, the amount increasing with the steepness of the flow and the velocity of the current. The same grit you trample underfoot en route to Mount Washburn's summit may eventually settle onto a shallow sandbar where herds of bison regularly ford a river. The rivers are the veins that pump life into Yellowstone.

The Yellowstone River has been flowing for at least two million years, all the while grinding, eroding, and forming its present course, which is by no means permanent. Geologists believe that the river achieved its present form about one hundred thousand years ago and took about seventy-five thousand years to gouge out the Grand Canyon of the Yellowstone. The current is still cutting deeper into the canyon, and the two falls, Upper and Lower, are creeping upstream toward Yellowstone Lake. But barring earthquakes or turmoils in this volcanic land, the Grand Canyon of the Yellowstone should look much the same in another one hundred thousand years as it does today.

One summer during the salad days of long ago I went searching for the source of the Yellowstone River, first on horseback and then on foot. Of course every river has many sources, tiny feeders or tributaries, but I was looking for the absolute farthest source, the beginning of the waterway that wanders 750 miles before

White pelicans cruise over a calm section of the Yellowstone River in Hayden Valley. At least a few are always present here in summer.

Thermals steam along the Yellowstone River between Yellowstone Lake and LeHardy Rapids. Nearby are Dragon's Mouth and Sulphur Caldron hot springs.

draining into the Missouri River near Sidney, Montana. I don't think I ever located the exact spot, which is somewhere on Yount's Peak southeast of the park, because my timing was bad and I found the area still covered with deep snow.

From its source the Yellowstone flows generally northward over a rolling, fairly open landscape, collecting the waters from Atlantic, Thorofare, and countless other smaller streams along the way. This is splendid wilderness country, bright green in early summer, turned golden by early October, unique in all the world at any season. By the time it enters Yellowstone Lake with water added from Escarpment, Mountain, Phlox, and Trapper's creeks, the Yellowstone is a major river. Within park boundaries a trail parallels the Yellowstone on the east side, but it sees little traffic.

Below Yellowstone Lake, altitude 7,733 feet, the Yellowstone River gradually picks up speed past LeHardy Rapids, Dragon's Mouth, and other mud geysers, past Sulphur Caldron Hot Springs, and into the Hayden Valley. The park's loop highway parallels this stretch of river on the west side, from spring through autumn providing a rare look into the past. Herds of bison roam as freely

here as they did before Europeans "discovered" the place. The August buffalo rut is an especially exciting, dusty event to watch. Flocks of Canada geese and other waterfowl gather along the banks and feed in the river, which is slow moving here.

Toward the north end of Hayden Valley, the Yellowstone again gathers speed and is deeper and darker. Pull off to the side of the pavement and you hear a roar in the distance. Out of sight the river plunges into the Grand Canyon, a gorge almost 1,500 feet deep. The roar comes from Upper Falls, an initial river drop of 109 feet that can be seen from several vantage points. Deeper into the Grand Canyon and a half mile farther along, the Yellowstone plunges another 308 feet over Lower Falls. Vistas of these from Artist Point, Inspiration Point, and other overlooks are possible all along the Grand Canyon's edge. Osprey soar over the canyon walls, which are a mineral blending of yellow, gray, pale green, brown, and pink. All the colors are deeper during mornings and evenings when the sun is low, or following a summertime squall.

Many times we have hiked the short distances from adjacent parking lots to Grand Canyon viewpoints, but

Otters live along most larger Yellowstone waterways. This young pair rests beside the Lamar River.

every time the view of the falls far below comes as a surprise. These are fine places to comprehend and hear the awesome force of nature. Try to blot out for a few minutes the other visitors that (except in very early morning) are probably standing around you, and it is almost like being present at the earth's creation.

The portion of the Yellowstone River from the Grand Canyon northward to near Tower Fall (where a highway bridge spans it) and from there northwestward to Gardiner, Montana, is not easily accessible. A few trails many miles apart lead to the river's edge, and narrow suspension bridges at Hellroaring Creek and in the Black Canyon allow hikers and horseback riders to cross into the purest wilderness country. Most of the few backpackers who roam this area try to keep it their own secret.

Whereas the eastern half of Yellowstone Park is drained by the Yellowstone River, a vast area of the western half is drained by the Gibbon and Firehole rivers, which merge to form the Madison River at Madison Junction. The Gibbon is a shallow stream that originates in Grebe Lake (near Canyon), meanders through Gibbon and Elk meadows where elk graze on warm summer evenings, and then hurries through Virginia Cascades and over Gibbon Falls. It was named for the army general, John Gibbon, who would later identify Custer's body at the Battle of Little Bighorn.

The Firehole is simply the most fantastic river, not only in Yellowstone Park, but perhaps anywhere. Along almost its entire length it collects runoff from the major thermal basins of the park. Mountain man Jim Bridger reported that the Firehole flowed so fast that the friction of the water against its bed heated the rocks beneath. That theory isn't quite as farfetched as it seems. In places the river bed at midstream *is* hot, but the high temperature is caused by hot springs seeping upward, not by friction. On cold mornings, the whole Firehole River steams, giving its valley a ghostly, surreal look and muffling sound. The trout simply avoid areas where hot waters are not diluted by the colder flow. It is an excellent trout fishery.

So is the Madison River, a classic trout stream from Madison Junction to Three Forks, Montana, where it joins the Gallatin River (also originating in Yellowstone) and the Beaverhead to form the Missouri River. If the Madison existed as a private trout stream in Europe, rather

Above: *A tolerant cow elk pauses midstream in the Madison River to allow a nearly full-grown calf to nurse.* **Left:** *A mallard drake in bright breeding colors emerges from the Yellowstone River to preen.*

than a public place in the United States, the daily fishing fees would exclude all but the wealthiest anglers.

Eleven species of fish were native to Yellowstone waters and five others have been introduced at various times to provide better fishing. Once the various high waterfalls prevented the movement of alien fishes upstream, and about one third of Yellowstone waters had no fish. That changed when the introduced species found homes where food and spawning sites were available. Yellowstone's cold, clear waters cannot be considered really rich, but they teem with the phytoplankton and zooplankton that are the basis of the aquatic food chain. Larvae of such insects as the abundant stoneflies feed on the plankton. The stoneflies are important in the diet of many stream fish. Mayflies, caddisflies, and dragonflies also thrive in Yellowstone waters.

Of the park's original native fishes, three were species of the salmon family. One, the arctic grayling, once fairly widespread, seems secure in a few small and remote Yellowstone ponds. Most numerous today, although its range has been greatly reduced to within the Yellowstone ecosystem, is the Yellowstone or black-spotted cutthroat trout, named for the red slash mark under its jaw. This is *the* trout species of Yellowstone Lake and of the Yellowstone River above the Grand Canyon. Cutthroat numbers today are high, especially in the lake, but certainly are not inexhaustible. During the last twenty years it has been necessary to carefully monitor the trout population and to restrict the anglers' catch by shortening the open season, by regulating the tackle used, and by encouraging catch-and-release fishing. During the early 1990s cutthroats were still the dominant fish species in the upper Yellowstone River and Yellowstone Lake.

Rainbow trout, brown trout, and lake trout have been introduced into Yellowstone Park waters in the past to provide more angling opportunity. Now rainbows and browns are the most important game species in the Madison River and some other park waters. But, fortunately for the native cutthroats, no rainbows or browns have yet invaded the upper Yellowstone River or the lake. However, two other aliens, the red-sided shiner (perhaps introduced illegally by fishermen as bait) and the longnose sucker have found their way into Yellowstone Lake. Both can in time furnish serious competition to cutthroats, the shiners by feeding on juvenile trout soon after they hatch, and the suckers by taking over traditional trout spawning areas. Yellowstone Lake cutthroats spawn in small feeder streams in early spring, and on a number of occasions I have watched grizzly bears catching them on the shallow riffles. Families of river otters are often seen feeding on spawning trout.

A fish tapeworm found in the Yellowstone River, in Heart Lake, and elsewhere also infests more than half of the cutthroat trout in Yellowstone Lake, apparently without harm. The key to the tapeworm's distribution is the numerous water birds of the region: ospreys and pelicans, gulls and cormorants. The worms lay eggs inside the host birds and the eggs are excreted into the water where they are eaten by small crustaceans that are then eaten by the trout. Once inside a cutthroat trout, tapeworm larvae bore through stomach walls into the flesh. This is the worm that anglers often find when dressing trout. The whole life cycle is completed when one of the birds, say a pelican, eats the trout plus the tapeworm, which then lays eggs in the pelican's body. The tapeworm is viewed as a normal, natural part of the ecosystem.

The introduction, deliberately or accidentally, of other exotic creatures into Yellowstone waters, however, is an ever-present threat to the ecosystem. Early in the 1980s it appeared that someone had released eastern brook trout into a Yellowstone Lake feeder stream. The results could have been disastrous, since it is known that this species, introduced to new territory, soon eliminates the natives. Park officials believe they have eliminated all eastern brook trout from Yellowstone waters.

Another ever-present danger is the eroding of stream banks and lake shores caused by the activities of too many anglers. In a few places along the Yellowstone River this has become a serious matter, and breaking down the banks has changed the character of the river. Even wading can be destructive. While trout populations can be regulated and preserved through enforced regulations, nothing much can be done once their habitat is degraded and lost. This concern is one all responsible anglers should keep in mind.

Above left: *Fall mists and a cottonwood dressed in autumn foliage rise from the bank of the Snake River near the park's south entrance.* **Above right:** *Hike out along the boardwalks from Old Faithful, and you'll pass many small, bubbling geysers such as this along the Firehole River.* **Left:** *Chocolate Pot is a boiling spring along the Gibbon River between Norris and Elk Meadow.*

Above: *About fifty pairs of ospreys nest each year in Yellowstone. The best place to see them is near the Grand Canyon of the Yellowstone River.* **Right:** *A pall of smoke and mist softens this scene of Gibbon Falls on the Gibbon River.*

In fall the Madison River valley is a scene of busy rutting activity. Here a bull elk follows his harem across the river.

The rare and endangered trumpeter swan, illuminated here by a summer sunset, is a common sight along the Madison River.

WINTER IN YELLOWSTONE

When winter descends on Yellowstone Country, most of the park is all but closed to human presence. A single roadway from Gardiner and Mammoth to Cooke City, Montana, is kept open to auto traffic. Snow closes other roads around November first, and they do not open again until May. Snowmobiles carry tourists from the community of West Yellowstone, Montana, from Mammoth, and from Flagg Ranch (near the South Entrance) into Snow Lodge, a winter accommodation at Old Faithful. Over-snow vehicles are restricted by law to the main loop roads. Except for a caretaker or two at Lake Hotel and Canyon Village, the central area of the park is empty of people from December through March. Now and then a very intrepid cross-country skier or a very dedicated scientist may poke into the backcountry, but that is all.

And no wonder. On the high Yellowstone plateau, temperatures as low as minus 70 degrees Fahrenheit have been recorded, according to the U.S. Weather Bureau. Temperatures may fall below even that. I remember one winter when nearly all activity ground to a halt in Jackson Hole, Wyoming, where we lived, as the mercury dropped to minus 60 degrees Fahrenheit for a few days. Snowfalls that begin in September in the heart of Yellowstone can add up to fifteen feet of snow over the winter. I have been caught in high-altitude snowstorms as late as mid-July.

To me the most amazing aspect of winter is how well the wild creatures are able to cope with it. For six

months in Yellowstone the margin between life and death is very thin. Some creatures do perish, but always enough survive to assure continuation of the species. Most birds fly south for the winter. Elk and mule deer migrate to lower elevations of the park and often out of it, some to the corridor between Yellowstone and Grand Teton national parks, others as far as the National Elk Refuge in Jackson Hole. Other species, from beavers and marmots to reptiles and jumping mice, hibernate. But all those that do not must contend with the most brutal weather conditions (outside of Alaska) in the United States.

The most astonishing example of survival is that of the dipper, or ouzel. Many of the streams where these birds live all summer are frozen solid in winter, so they move to the few streams that continue to flow, warmed by the thermal activity nearby. One morning in early March when the air temperature hovered between minus 15 and minus 20 degrees Fahrenheit, and my fingers were too stiff with the cold to handle a camera, I watched two dippers repeatedly plunge into the swift Gardner River, which was frozen along its fringes. After a few moments the birds would reappear on the bank long enough to shed water from their feathers before diving in again. Evidently the dippers find enough food to provide the energy they need. It could be that aquatic insects are slower moving and easier to catch when the water temperature is near freezing.

All of the active winter residents of Yellowstone must prepare well during summer and autumn for the com-

Winter is a critical time for Yellowstone elk. This bull is wintering near Beryl Spring along the Gibbon River.

Peggy Bauer skis along the Firehole River, near Old Faithful, just after a winter blizzard.

ing ordeal. Bears spend the summer in a search for food that may add a four-inch layer of fat to their bodies before they begin their six-month sleep. From August onward hikers may come upon piles of grass and herbs drying, curing in the sun, wherever the trail crosses rock slides or boulder fields. These miniature haystacks, some as big as bushel baskets, are the winter food supplies for pikas and pocket gophers, who do not hibernate. We have spent far too many hours on warm and magic September afternoons just watching the busy pikas gathering their "crops," carrying mouthfuls of grass from long distances on short legs to add to the stack. Once through binoculars we saw a black bear suddenly appear and in a few seconds gulp down a pika's entire winter store.

In preparation for winter, ruffed and blue grouse, red foxes and coyotes, prey and their predators, grow additional feathers or hair on their feet, both to reduce heat loss and to act somewhat as snowshoes, spreading their weight over a larger area and allowing easier going over the snow. After molting, all species grow heavier winter coats. Some of these new winter coats are white rather than the brown worn in summer. Those that change color include whitetail jackrabbits, snowshoe (or

varying) hares, and short-tailed weasels.

The white pelage is good camouflage against the snow and therefore some protection from the keen vision of predators, especially from birds of prey. But the color can also be a distinct disadvantage during those years when the molt to white begins before the snows fall, or lingers after an early thaw. We have photographed white or nearly white jackrabbits when the first sage buttercups were blooming in early spring.

Few species of birds remain on the Yellowstone plateau for the duration of winter. But those that do—Canada jays, chickadees, nuthatches, ravens, magpies, and Clark's nutcrackers to list a few—add more feathers. Whenever at rest, the feathers are fluffed out to improve their insulating properties.

The large mammals cope in various ways, mainly by moving around as little as possible and thereby saving precious calories. Elk take advantage of the winter sun on south-facing slopes whenever possible. At night and when daytimes are windy, they are likely to move into forests to spare heat loss. In Yellowstone elk and moose enjoy one advantage that doesn't exist elsewhere to help take the cruel edge off winter: the hot thermal areas. I

Dusk comes early in January. At Norris Geyser Basin, steam has crystallized on the trees, giving them grotesquely beautiful shapes.

have seen elk and bison lying on bare ground and crowding close to the steam vents and hot springs for warmth. Although this must be pleasant, it doesn't help much in the animal's winter-long struggle against starvation. The big herbivores often must dig and paw through deep snow in search of food; what little they find is usually of poor quality. All the grasses that are rich in carbohydrates and proteins during summer store their nutrients underground in winter.

At least once each winter, with cross-country skis on the roof rack and snow tires on the car wheels, we make the drive from home through Mammoth (where a few elk winter on the fertilized lawn surrounding park headquarters) and onward through Roosevelt to Cooke City, Montana. It is a scenic day-long drive during the peak tourist months, but during the off-season it is the best chance to see close-up how wild creatures survive the deep snow country. Many buffaloes spend the winter right along this road through the Lamar Valley. They spend a good bit of time bedded down, conserving energy. If a polar air mass sweeps down and blowing snow drifts completely cover the animals, they still may not move for long periods until some inner clock or hunger

indicator urges them to action.

Early one dazzlingly bright, sub-zero morning, following a heavy overnight snowfall, my friend and fellow photographer Bill Browning and I drove slowly up the Lamar Valley road toward Cooke. Winter traffic is very light and this morning no others cars had preceded us. Even with 4-wheel-drive we were extremely cautious. We had hoped to find and photograph the several large bighorn rams that were wintering around Soda Butte. All at once, rounding a bend, Bill hit the brakes and swerved sharply to avoid hitting a buffalo that suddenly appeared, ghostlike, in our path. It had been bedded in the middle of the road and was completely covered by the snowfall of the previous night.

In the next few seconds we watched in disbelief as, one by one, about forty other buffalos appeared from beneath the sheet of pure white all around us. Almost leisurely the shaggy dark animals stood up and shook the snow from their backs before moving slowly away, like a battalion of tanks. Not far from the Lamar River's edge they began to feed, swinging their heavy heads to excavate into the snow for the forage below.

At least one of the animals in that herd did not find

On a minus-twenty-degree morning, animal tracks are etched in new snow along the Madison River. Elk and bison herds winter here.

Near Upper Geyser Basin, a bison stands motionless in winter to conserve heat and energy during the intensely cold days.

enough to eat. Two days later, with the rest of the herd standing about a quarter of a mile away, we saw the carcass being ripped open by a trio of coyotes. Ravens and a pair of eagles also were on the scene.

Not even the clever, adaptable coyotes have an easy time surviving winter, which may be a season of great feasting or of famine, depending on the winter kill of other creatures. Coyotes have a tough time moving through the deep, soft snow that is a cinch for bison or moose. But biologists have found that coyotes use their brains as much as their four feet when hunting. Instinctively or visually they somehow "read" the character of the snow ahead. Clearly coyotes try to avoid soft snow altogether and proceed carefully over "medium" snow, always trying to avoid breaking through a thin crust. Whenever possible they keep to wind-packed surfaces where they can run down prey when it flushes. However, coyotes always choose soft snow for bedding places. And they seem to know if the snow covering a meadow is soft enough to make a head-first dive for the rodents scurrying underneath.

On another trip into the Lamar Valley, in search of the same bighorn rams, I learned in one split second how vital it is to be able to "read" snow. Not far from Soda Butte, Peggy and I found the fresh tracks of sheep leading up a steep slope to where they had bedded down on a sunny ledge. I grabbed a camera with telephoto lens and began to follow the switch-backed ram's trail toward a good photographic viewpoint. Halfway up the slope I saw that I could take a shortcut and avoid the longer hairpin curve the sheep had made. I turned that way—but it was a big mistake. Next thing I knew I had lost my footing and was flying upside down to the bottom of the slope. The camera bumped along beside me. Although I was only bruised, my photo gear was smashed beyond use. I had tried to cross a sheet of ice lying under the snow that the rams had instinctively avoided, and I nearly became a winter statistic myself because of it.

Hunting is not allowed in Yellowstone Park. Thus, the coyote population here is fairly high, and they live more natural lives than they do in cattle-raising country.

Here coyotes often hunt in packs, probably extended family groups. They pull down an occasional elk calf in spring, but in winter will also prey on large bulls that enter the hunger moon with low fat and energy reserves after a hectic breeding season.

Parasites as well as coyotes prey on large mammals throughout winter. We once watched a male elk on the National Elk Refuge die slowly over days (probably weeks) because it was infested with the mites or mange. Toward the end it was rendered nearly bald as chunks of its hair fell out, littering the snow around its last bed. Coyotes were always near this bull but did not approach it until the carcass was stiff and cold.

Winter ticks can also be a terrible nuisance to mammals. They infect moose and elk to such an extent that the snowy white beds of the animals are reddened with blood—caused by the big ungulates shifting position, crushing ticks that are engorged with their blood.

But it is more likely an exquisite, magnificent, steaming landscape than a sick moose that a visitor is likely to find on a mid-winter holiday in Yellowstone. Take the daily snowcoach from the little town of West Yellowstone, Montana, on the west border of the park, and ride along the Madison River toward Old Faithful. Carry along your cross-country skis or rent them at Snow Lodge. Plan to spend at least several days to insure including a few sunny days, and it will be a winter holiday unique in all the world.

From the lodge it is an easy, pleasant, go-at-your-own-pace glide up or down the Firehole River. Ski out to and through the Upper Geyser Basin to Morning Glory Pool, Castle Geyser, Sapphire Pool, and the other geothermals. The place will be ghostly and strange, a blue and white world that summer-only visitors cannot at first believe. Unlike the wildlife that you will meet along the ski trails, you can add or subtract layers of clothing as the weather dictates. Day's end back at warm Snow Lodge is always a very delicious time.

I am always happy to see April and May and springtime return to Yellowstone, but I know I am lucky to have seen so many winters there, too.

Coyotes are the easiest of the park's carnivores to spot.
They're most often seen in the Lamar Valley in winter.

Above: *Hoar frost on quaking aspen trees is illuminated by a low winter sun.* **Left:** *A midwinter scene shows the path of the Lamar River as it leaves its broad, flat valley and enters Lamar Canyon.* **Right:** *Throughout winter, the tracks they leave behind are the best evidence that cougars live wherever prey animals are concentrated in the park.*

EPILOGUE

Late in the springtime of 1992 Steve and Marilynn French watched a gathering of grizzly bears feeding together in a remote amphitheater, high in the Absaroka Mountains looming over Yellowstone Park's east boundary. It was strange to find so many of the normally ungregarious animals in a group. But stranger still was the fare: The grizzlies were not dining on the succulent, new green grass or on the carcass of a winter-killed elk. Instead, the Wyoming husband and wife researchers noted, the bears were licking up the hosts of army cuttworm moths that migrate here each summer to feed on the nectar of alpine wildflowers. These insects may be a higher source of energy, pound for pound, than anything else in the bear's diet.

But the Frenches' discovery had far greater significance than just the bears' insect diet. Only a generation ago the ancestors of these grizzlies were living on the bounty they found in park garbage dumps. Almost five thousand tons of garbage, mostly food scraps, are left behind by Yellowstone Park visitors every summer. It was generally conceded that most Yellowstone bears had forgotten how to forage in any other way. They had come to depend on the dumps as a food source just as their cousins the Alaskan brown bears depend on spawning salmon.

After the dumps were closed in 1970, many bears had to be eliminated when they invaded public campgrounds and scavenged in the waste pits of surrounding towns. Suddenly the grizzlies were considered a danger-ous nuisance, and their numbers dropped to an all-time low. Many wildlife biologists doubted that these Yellowstone bears could ever return to their old, natural ways. Now those same biologists are happy that they may have been proven wrong.

No one can explain why or how the grizzlies re-learned their old habits, but it might be a crash course in Darwinism. Not only are the bears harvesting the bumper crop of cuttworm moths, but they are again capturing young elk on the May/June calving grounds, fishing for spawning cutthroat trout, and digging in summertime for such nutritious wild plants as biscuitroot. At least for the time being the Yellowstone grizzly bear population seems secure and healthy.

In early August 1992 another important incident occurred in the Yellowstone backcountry, and this one was recorded by a commercial film crew. At daybreak one morning the crew focused on a pair of adult grizzly bears ripping into the carcass of a bison. Nearby were twin bear cubs, gamboling, and a coyote that had already gorged on the bison. Ravens circled overhead. But suddenly the camera operators were astounded to see another dark, long-legged animal, larger than a coyote, in the viewfinder. The blackish mystery animal could have been a domesticated wolf or a dog-wolf hybrid abandoned by its owner. (Many such hybrids exist as pets in the West.) But its furtive stance and behavior around the bears all but convinced experts who saw the film that it was a genuine wild gray wolf. Furthering the

Geologists believe that it has taken the Yellowstone River 160,000 years to carve this deep gorge below Lower Falls.

biologists' opinion was the knowledge that wolves have been slowly moving southward from Canada and Glacier National Park in Montana, where at least four packs or sixty individuals are now living free.

More than a month later, a second incident triggered concerns for a wolf-inhabited Yellowstone. On September 30, 1992, a group of elk hunters shot an animal they believed was a coyote in the Bridger-Teton National Forest, which is just outside Yellowstone's southern boundary. On finding that the animal was not a coyote, the hunters notified park rangers, who packed out the carcass two days later. They then shipped the ninety-two pound, black and silver-grizzled animal— what park wildlife biologists believed to be a gray wolf— to the U.S. Fish and Wildlife Service forensic laboratory in Ashland, Oregon, for positive identification.

This animal may or may not have been the same one filmed among the bears' bison kill in Hayden Valley forty miles to the north. But if indeed the animal was a wolf, it does offer further evidence that wolves can disperse the three hundred miles from Glacier into Yellowstone. Judging from the animal's teeth, the dead "wolf" was a young one and was about the right age to seek out its own territory.

All at once it seems possible that future Yellowstone visitors might be serenaded by wild wolves howling on cool nights. But the shooting suggests how difficult it will be for an old native to live again in the Yellowstone wilderness. And even if the filmed wolf survives, one wolf does not translate into a pack until a mate somehow is found.

Nevertheless, there is some optimism that Yellowstone Park, like its grizzly bears, is in good health and unthreatened. But remember that both the large bears and the wolves are great wanderers. A male grizzly can rove across one thousand square miles and far beyond park boundaries. Although the Endangered Species Act requires that the habitat of grizzly bears and wolves (as well as that of other endangered species) be managed to assure their survival, it is no match for the pressure from mining, timber harvesting, and livestock grazing interests that demand the same land for their own purposes. Even as I write, in early fall 1992, the president and vice president of the United States are busy trying to eviscerate the Endangered Species Act. And the future of Yellowstone itself is far from certain, given the priorities of too many politicians today.

In 1980 the Office of Science and Technology of the National Park Service finished the first comprehensive survey that identified threats to the natural resources of all our national parks. The findings were generally sobering and bleak, especially for Yellowstone, and threats to the park have not decreased in the decade or so since the report was issued. The greatest internal threat is too many people loving the park to death with not nearly enough money appropriated by Congress to cope with it.

But the truth is that most of the threats and degradation of Yellowstone are caused by activities and sources located outside the park boundaries. A partial list of these includes logging, mining, oil and gas exploration, cattle over-grazing, poaching, destruction of wildlife habitat, soil erosion, water and air pollution, unnecessary roads, noise, off-road vehicle use, subdivisions for housing and strip malls, and encroachment of exotic plants and animals. Consider a few specific examples.

A Canadian mining company, Noranda Inc., has plans for a mine estimated to contain 680 million dollars worth of gold in the Beartooth Mountains just northeast of Yellowstone Park; a myriad of other companies would like to follow suit. Officials of the Shoshone National Forest appear ready to permit oil exploration in the vicinity of scenic Brooks Lake and the Du Noir area just southeast of Yellowstone. They also have proposed timber sales on over thirty-one thousand acres in that same Du Noir area, which is important grizzly bear habitat. One Forest Service biologist, Bob Hitchcock, resigned in protest. "[Forest Service officials] need to take a breather," he said, "with no logging and no development whatever for thirty or forty years."

A point on the bright side is the fact that such environmental groups as the Sierra Club, the Wilderness Society, and the Greater Yellowstone Coalition are constant, alert watchdogs against all the planned development.

The biggest problem *within* Yellowstone Park is similar to that facing the entire planet: too many people. The number of visitors grows annually while the federal funding to manage all of them becomes harder to obtain from Congress. At times during midsummer, Yellowstone roads and facilities become so crowded that enjoyment of the park is difficult. Many solutions have been offered to solve the problem, from restricting private auto traffic or replacing it altogether with a public shuttle system (as in Yosemite and Denali national parks), to the extreme of removing all facilities of every kind and returning the park to pure wilderness status.

It is certainly true that some unsightly structures and unnecessary services could be removed. Surely there should be a strict ban on future additional development. But there are dangers in drastic restrictions or cutbacks to what has become the traditional use of Yellowstone. I do not believe that the wildlife is unduly disturbed by people pressure. Much of the Yellowstone backcountry is as silent and magnificent as when I first explored beyond the pavements over a half century ago. Only the areas burned in 1988 are sad and unpleasant to revisit.

In order to be long and lovingly preserved, any national treasure needs strong and enthusiastic citizen support. Yellowstone is no exception. Unfortunately, the public is unlikely to support a faraway park it cannot ever hope to see or enjoy. To keep people involved in what happens at Yellowstone, informed, educated use of the park must be encouraged, rather than restricting use. We must preserve Yellowstone's original purpose as "a pleasuring ground for the benefit and enjoyment of the people."

To me Yellowstone will always be the world's premier national park, in more ways than having been the first so named.

Overleaf: This gray wolf was photographed in northern Montana, not in Yellowstone. But it someday it may be possible to see this native again in the park.

READINGS

Bauer, Erwin A. *Bear in Their World.* New York: Outdoor Life Books, 1985.

——. *Horned and Antlered Game.* New York: Outdoor Life Books, 1986.

——. *Photographing the North American West.* Seattle: Pacific Search Press and Globe Pequot Press, 1987.

Bryan, T. Scott. *The Geysers of Yellowstone.* Boulder, CO: University of Colorado Press, 1991.

Carter, Tom. *Day Hiking Yellowstone.* Garland, TX: Trails Illustrated, 1991.

McEneaney, Terry. *Birds of Yellowstone.* Boulder, CO: Roberts Rinehart, 1988.

Marshall, Mark C. *Yellowstone Trails, a Hiking Guide.* The Yellowstone Association, 1990.

Northern Rockies Conservation Cooperative. *Rare, Sensitive, and Threatened Species of the Greater Yellowstone Ecosystem.* Jackson, WY, 1989.

Schullery, Paul. *Yellowstone Bear Tales.* New York: William Morrow, 1991.

——. *Old Yellowstone Days.* Boulder, CO: Colorado Associated University Press, 1979.

Shaw, Richard J. *Wildflowers of Grand Teton and Yellowstone National Parks.* Salt Lake City: Wheelwright Press, 1991.

——. *Plants of Yellowstone and Grand Teton National Parks.* Salt Lake City: Wheelwright Press, 1981.

Sholly, Dan R. *Guardians of Yellowstone.* New York: William Morrow, 1991.

Sutton, Ann and Myron Sutton. *Yellowstone—A Century of the Wilderness Idea.* New York: Macmillan Company, 1972.

ABOUT THE BAUERS

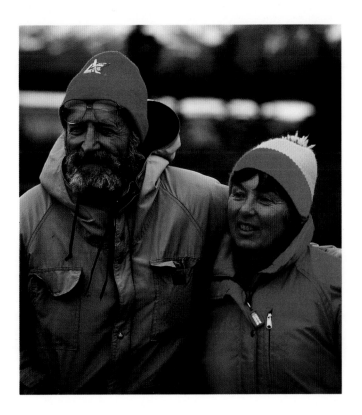

Erwin and Peggy Bauer are busy, full-time photographers and writers of travel, adventure, and environmental subjects. Based in Paradise Valley, Montana, the Bauers have specialized in photographing wildlife worldwide for over forty years. Their images come from the Arctic to the Antarctic; Borneo to Brazil; Africa; India; and remote places you may never have heard of.

The Bauers' recent magazine credits include *Natural History, Outdoor Life, Audubon, National Geographic, Smithsonian, Wildlife Conservation, National Wildlife* and *International Wildlife, Sierra, Safari, Chevron USA,* and *Nature Conservancy.* Their photographs annually illustrate the calendars of the Sierra Club, the Audubon Society, World Wildlife Fund, and others. The Bauers have a dozen books currently in print, including *Whitetails: Behavior, Ecology, Conservation,* also published by Voyageur Press. The couple has won awards for wildlife photography in national and international photographic competitions. Erwin and Peggy Bauer may be the most frequently published wildlife photographers in the world today.